The Domain of the Novel

The Domain of the Novel: Reflections on Some Historical Definitions discusses the genre of the novel and its dialogic and dialectical characteristics through an in-depth analysis of some classic English, Russian, American and Indian novels. A collection of lectures by the distinguished scholar of literature A. N. Kaul, it analyzes the exploration of personal voices and histories within a larger socio-political landscape in these works.

Drawing examples from the works of Fielding, George Eliot, Dickens, Thackeray, Melville, Hawthorne, Twain, R.K. Narayan and others who defined and redefined the territories of the novel, this book examines the articulation of the lived social, political and material realities of ordinary individuals in this genre. The lectures situate the novels within their cultural, socio-political and historical contexts while focussing on their historical continuity and relevance. They further demonstrate how the domain of the novel brings together a multitude of voices while discussing conflicts of class, identity, nationalism and historiography.

The volume includes an insightful critical introduction by Sambudha Sen. It will be of great interest to researchers and scholars of literature, cultural studies, post-colonial studies, literary theory, creative writing, history and sociology. It will be especially useful for readers interested in studying forms of fiction and the 18th-, 19th- and 20th-century novel.

A. N. Kaul (1930–2017), Rhodes Scholar, B.Litt. (Oxon), Fulbright and Rockefeller Fellow, Ph.D. in American Studies (Yale). His dissertation, *The American Vision: Actual and Ideal Society in Nineteenth-Century Fiction*, won both the John Addison Porter and George Egleston History Prizes and was published by Yale University Press in 1963. Considered a path-breaking study, it continues to be relevant. Apart from articles and reviews, he is the author of *The Action of English Comedy: Studies in the Encounter of Abstraction and Experience from Shakespeare to Shaw* (1970) and *History, Sociology and the American Romance* (1990); and he edited *Hawthorne* in the 20th Century Views series (1966). He had a distinguished teaching career. Starting at Delhi College (now Zakir Hussain College), University of Delhi, he was Associate Professor of English and American Studies at Yale, and, deciding to return to India, Professor (and Head for several years) of English at the University of Delhi and, later, Pro-Vice-Chancellor. He was Visiting Professor at the Indian Institute of Advanced Study, Shimla, the University of Kashmir, Sir George Williams (now Concordia) University, Montreal, the University of Texas at Austin on two separate occasions and Oberlin College, Ohio. He moved permanently to Edmonton, Alberta, in 2012.

Sambudha Sen is Professor and Head, Department of English, Shiv Nadar University, and studied at the University of Delhi, where his doctoral work was on Charles Dickens, and he taught there for several years becoming Professor and Head, Department of English, before moving to his present position. He has held fellowships, among other places, at Cambridge University, Bellagio, the Huntingdon Library and Columbia University, and been Visiting Professor at Jadavpur and Calcutta Universities. He has published widely, articles on the 18th and 19th century novel in *Nineteenth Century Literature* and *Victorian Studies,* and a book, *Radical Expression and the Making of the Dickensian Aesthetic* (2012).

Mythili Kaul is a retired Professor and former Head, Department of English, University of Delhi, having taught there throughout her career. Her doctoral work at Yale was on Shakespeare's Romances, and she has published articles on Shakespeare in national and international journals and edited *Othello: New Essays by Black Writers* (1997).

'Professor A. N. Kaul's essays are deeply-informed, wide-ranging critiques of novelistic practices, as well as of critical approaches to them. They represent Professor Kaul at his humane, insightful, sparkling best, and this volume is a wonderful testimonial to his legendary pedagogy.'

Suvir Kaul, *A. M. Rosenthal Professor, Department of English, University of Pennsylvania*

'These four posthumous essays by Professor A. N. Kaul constitute a treasure-trove of immensely important reflections on the formation of the novel. They traverse early novels and their self-understandings across several continents and centuries maintaining the integrity of each while effortlessly weaving diverse contexts and works into a unified literary realm. The essays bring together the individual/domestic and the political/ideological that went into the novel's making in different ways and with different meanings. They also trace their genesis in, and overlaps with, other literary and discursive Genres. The luminous prose of the essays recalls the best of the novelists.'

Tanika Sarkar, *Retired Professor, Modern History, Jawaharlal Nehru University, Delhi*

'The previously unpublished essays of A. N. Kaul are like gifts from one of the most insightful, imaginative, and distinctive interpreters of Hawthorne and his generation. Reading these thoughtful essays is like being freed from chilly and disenchanted days by a warm, optimistic, and consistently incisive critic whose lyrical writing and generous intelligence represents the best of a classic era of American literary criticism. Accessible and fascinating, these essays will charm and enlighten any enthusiast of fiction from a wide range of periods and places.'

Christopher Castiglia, *author of* The Practices of Hope: Literary Criticism in Disenchanted Times, *Distinguished Professor of English, Pennsylvania State University, Pennsylvania*

The Domain of the Novel
Reflections on Some Historical
Definitions

A. N. Kaul
Introduction by Sambudha Sen

Routledge
Taylor & Francis Group

LONDON AND NEW YORK

First published 2021
by Routledge
2 Park Square, Milton Park, Abingdon, Oxon OX14 4RN

and by Routledge
52 Vanderbilt Avenue, New York, NY 10017

*Routledge is an imprint of the Taylor & Francis Group, an informa
business*

British Library Cataloguing-in-Publication Data
A catalogue record for this book is available from the British
Library

Library of Congress Cataloging-in-Publication Data
Names: Kaul, A. N., author.
Title: The domain of the novel : reflections on some historical
    definitions / A. N. Kaul.
Description: New York : Routledge, 2020. | Includes
    bibliographical references and index.
Identifiers: LCCN 2020028256 (print) | LCCN 2020028257
    (ebook)
Subjects: LCSH: Fiction—History and criticism. | Literature and
    society. | Literature and history.
Classification: LCC PN3491 .K326 2020 (print) | LCC PN3491
    (ebook) | DDC 808.3—dc23
LC record available at https://lccn.loc.gov/2020028256
LC ebook record available at https://lccn.loc.gov/2020028257

ISBN: 978-0-367-90129-5 (hbk)
ISBN: 978-1-003-02548-1 (ebk)

Typeset in Times New Roman
by Apex CoVantage, LLC

For the generations of students who heard him and
will hear him through these lectures

Contents

Foreword

Professor Kaul delivered these lectures twenty years ago at Sri Venkateswara College, University of Delhi. It took Ahmer Anwer, Pradip Datta and Sambudha Sen, former students, then colleagues and friends, several visits and discussions to persuade him to agree to them and they are the 'onelie begetters' of the present volume.

Professor Kaul was a great communicator and a legendary teacher, and these lectures show him at his best – his deep engagement with his chosen field, the humanities, and a lifetime of reading, thinking and teaching. Teaching, he often said, helped him to clarify his ideas and his cardinal principles in teaching and writing were clarity and lucidity. In one of the lectures he tells the Chairperson that he 'would sacrifice "comprehensiveness" for "comprehensibility"'', and that is precisely what he demonstrates in these pages. He was always abreast of current developments and the latest critical terminology but avoided jargon and fashionable phrases and advised his students to do the same. He was at pains, as can be seen, to define, explain and elucidate the concepts and terms he used.

The novel was his 'domain', and these lectures reveal his mastery over it. Over the years he said that he would like to write a book called *The House of Fiction* which would deal with the English, American, Russian and Indian novel. He did not write the book, but *The Domain of the Novel* comes close, covering as it does these very fields. He was dissatisfied with his treatment of the Indian novel. He was well-up in Urdu and Hindi novels (which he read in Urdu) but felt that he could not do justice to them without going into their distinctive background and placing them, as he did the other works with which he was dealing, in their context, which would need at the very least a separate lecture. The expatriate novelists did not quite fit the subject, and he therefore confined himself to R.K. Narayan, whom he admired.

The Domain of the Novel shows the sweep that is characteristic of all he said and wrote. He did not think small; his thinking was, in the words of

one of his favourite poets, 'large' and contained 'multitudes'. He invariably saw literary works in the round, as it were, and felt that they could
be best understood when approached 'through the surrounding interactive
domains of history, society and politics'. What is striking is the remark-
able originality of the insights he brought to texts that are well-known and
well-rehearsed. He deliberately selected as the focus of these lectures 'old
and old-fashioned novels' and succeeded in revealing their freshness and
relevance. He subscribed to the position that all great works and writers are
great because they have stood the test of time and are perennially relevant,
are not of an age but for all time, and that every generation discovers this
relevance for itself.

I transcribed the lectures from Professor Kaul's notes and, in the case of
the lectures on the English novel and Ideology, I had cassettes as well, so
I was able to synthesize the notes and the cassettes. The lecture on Hawthorne was delivered much earlier but fits the general rubric and is therefore
included. I had difficulties with its transcription: there were no notes for that
lecture, only a cassette in which he was speaking so fast that, despite playing it over and over, I was unsuccessful in getting anything down. However,
Linda Jorgenson of Calgary, Alberta, was able to do what I could not, and
I am very grateful to her for doing such a thorough, professional job in tran-
scribing the lecture and making it accessible.

I am glad of the cassettes because I was able to *hear* the lectures, and going
through the written transcripts, it seems to me that his speaking voice comes
through. Retaining that voice has been the purpose, and I hope the Notes and
Works Cited sections do not interfere with or take away from that effect.

I owe a debt of gratitude to Anwer and Sambudha for seeing this project through. Anwer was very generous with his time, replied promptly to
my queries and provided the necessary clarifications, and I benefited from
his comments on each lecture as it was transcribed. Sambudha encouraged
publication and readily agreed to write the Introduction. Both of them knew
Professor Kaul and his work better than almost anyone else and stayed in
touch with him, and I am glad they have been involved with this book.

I must also acknowledge the encouragement and support of Professor
Rupin Desai, colleague and close friend of many decades, with whom Professor Kaul shared an abiding interest in Emerson, Thoreau and Yeats.

I could not have hoped for a better editor than Shoma Choudhury. I was
delighted with her positive response when I first submitted the book pro-
posal, and she continues to be positive as well as prompt in replying to all
queries. She is extremely accommodating and flexible, and her suggestions
have helped to clarify and smooth out problems. It has been a pleasure to
work with her and Shloka Chauhan, and I wish to thank her and Shloka
Chauhan for all they have done.

I also wish to thank the staff of the Rutherford Library of the University of Alberta, not only for their unfailing cheerfulness but for going out of their way to assist in tracking down references and sources, even to the extent of downloading articles and emailing them to me.

I must confess that the ways of computers mystify me, and time and again members of my family, mostly Padma and recently Sahara, have had to extricate me from the problems I have created. Padma also formatted the manuscript. I am grateful to her and to Sahara, to Aditya and Sidhartha for their suggestions and emendations and to all of them – Aditya, Padma, Sidhartha and Joni – for their help and encouragement and for the interest they have shown throughout this project. And to Sahara and Neva for the brightness and happiness they brought with themselves when they arrived, especially for their grandfather. I am glad they knew him.

Mythili Kaul
Edmonton, Canada
March 1, 2020

Introduction

Sambudha Sen

Reading transcripts of these lectures on the novel by Professor Kaul, delivered over two decades ago, I had the impression that like Ricardo Reis, the
sad, thoughtful and quietly brilliant protagonist of Jose Saramago's great
novel, Professor Kaul had come back from the dead. This impression had
nothing to do with the illusion that eloquent words make men live eternally.
Professor Kaul understood with greater clarity, tolerance and good humour
than most that literary arguments, like every form of human expression,
are historically constituted and therefore always liable to be overtaken by
history. Rather, it was the lingering echo of his speaking voice in these
written-up lectures that seemed somehow to bring him back. I imagined him
smelling the repression in the air as soon as he stepped back into the world,
like Ricardo Reis did when he entered Salazar's Lisbon after an absence
of several years. And then, just like Reis began that conversation with Fer-
nando Pessoa – his alter ego, who also happened to be Portugal's greatest
poet – I imagined Kaul looking curiously at his lectures – committed to
print by the immense persistence of his wife, Mythili Kaul – and wondering
what a new generation of students, teachers and scholars would make of
them and if – since he never wrote a word that was not capable of holding
its own on the international stage – his ideas continued to resonate with the
field of novel theory as it has developed through the last two decades.

Professor Kaul gave the three talks that appear in this volume in December 1998, a few years after he'd retired from Delhi University. It had taken
us considerable effort to persuade him to come out of retirement for three
days and address his many admirers. Even after he'd agreed, he asked me
at one point to put everything on hold because he did not know where those
lectures were taking him. Anyone who's seen Professor Kaul make a presentation or read a page of his published work would know the intelligence
and ease with which he conducted himself on any academic stage. So many
of us found his hesitancy over three simple lectures incomprehensible. It
was only during his first address, when he staked out the ground he planned

to cover in the lecture series, that we became aware of the scope of what Kaul was about to do.

Specifically, Kaul seemed to be attempting nothing less than a synthesis of a lifetime's work on the novel. He committed himself early, in his opening lecture, to engaging with the vast range of predominantly 19th-century novels with which he'd worked through the course of his entire career: the 19th-century English novels that he taught at the master's level, the work of Puskhin, Lermontov and Goncharov on which he'd led some brilliant M.Phil seminars, some English language fiction from 20th-century India that had begun to interest him and the 19th-century American novel – a field in which he was one of the world's leading authorities. The lectures went brilliantly. All three attracted huge audiences made up of Professor Kaul's colleagues from the English Department, students and, most of all, teachers from the colleges of Delhi University whom he had taught at some point in his life. He managed, from the moment he walked to the podium for the first lecture, to create that magically relaxed atmosphere that had always been the trademark of his classes. But he also held everyone spellbound. Every example he picked from his vast knowledge of novels was exact, he packed more insights into a single sentence than most people manage in three pages and he communicated his ideas with a scintillating clarity that only he was capable of. And yes, some of us were struck by his sustained and critical engagement with the 'ideology criticism' that Louis Althusser's work had spawned in American Studies. Indeed, I remember loudly proclaiming at a party after the lectures that A. N. Kaul had done for literary critics what E.P. Thompson had done for historians: retrieved the space for experience and its capacity to transform from the ironclad determinism of Althusser's thought.

But that was it. We preserved tapes of the lectures and agreed that they should be published. But no one really took the initiative, and over the years as the lectures receded into the past, they took on, in my mind at least, the status of legendary events that would only suffer defilement if exposed to the scrutiny of a world that had changed dramatically in many ways. Then Professor Kaul passed away on December 11, 2017. Mrs. Kaul turned to the Venkateswara tapes, worked diligently at them until she'd brought them to a publishable form and, after securing Routledge to act as publisher, she asked me to write the Introduction.

Naturally, it was an honour to be offered the opportunity to introduce the last great lectures of a man who not only transformed my thinking and ways of working through the course of shepherding me through a PhD, but who also happened to be among the greatest teachers of English literature to have worked in India. Taking into account that many saw the lectures as the culmination of a legendary career, I thought I'd write about Professor Kaul's

outstanding qualities as a teacher and the spread and depth of English studies in Delhi University and its colleges that he had helped to sustain before
it all fell apart. I thought, that is, I'd write about the past.

But from the moment I began reading the manuscript, I realized Professor
Kaul's lectures were not what I'd thought them to be. It was not so much that
I discovered in them things that I had forgotten. Rather, what jumped out
from the printed text was a certain animation – the animation of Professor
Kaul's speaking voice, of course, humorous, relaxed yet completely
confident – but also something more – something new that spoke to the
present. That is when I thought that like Ricardo Reis, Professor Kaul had
stepped back into life: sad, aloof, very far from the cheerful teacher he used
to be but unable to resist the tug of life, because like the fragments of Pessoa's verse that float up to Reis's mind, Kaul's thoughts on the novel seemed
to resonate more than ever before with some of the central preoccupations
of novel theory as it has developed over the last three decades.

Kaul's project in *The Domain of the Novel* is to uncover the multiple and
complicated ways by which the novel achieved the two breakthroughs with
which it revolutionized the world of letters. These were, as Catherine Gallagher put it in a 2006 essay, 'to taxonomize the social body and individu-
alize the character'.[1] However, even before it set about taxonomizing the
social body, the novel had to discursively produce the social. This domain
had never stabilized in the epic which, as Guido Mazzoni has argued, 'bore
the weight but not the details of a community' or in the mood driven, often
exotic settings of the Greek romances. On the other hand, Kaul argues, as
Thomas Pavel and Mazzoni have more recently, that the novel acquired a
crucial element in its self-definition when it began embedding narrative in
a densely detailed external world in which every element was immediately
recognizable as a reflection of the real.[2] Once installed within the novel, the
social became both an object of analysis and the novel's central dynamic,
determining the limits within which its plot could be made to unfold, the
types of objects that could circulate within it and the trajectories along
which its characters could be made to develop. It also became the ground on
which authors could inscribe their sense of the nation: sometimes integra-
tive and inward looking, at others conflicted by pressures from the outside
and, finally, revolutionary, aimed at destabilizing the basic organizational
principles of the social itself.

The Domain of the Novel also focuses on the novel's relationship with
a second figure of modernity – the lifelike individual. Like Thomas Pavel,
Kaul argues that in order to gain interiority and depth – the qualities that
made it lifelike – the novelistic character had to separate him/herself from
the superhuman hero of the epic as well as what recent criticism has designated as the 'ideographic' figure who embodied a virtue or vice in allegories

and moral parables. But what Pavel calls 'the enchantment of interiority' did not, in Kaul's account, free itself from either the moral abstractions of allegories or the longing for epic possibilities until late in the 19th century.³ Still, Kaul shows that the modern novelistic character moved increasingly away from the moral universe of the allegory or the vast supernatural stage of the epic to the domain of the social, and it is in tracking the complicated and varied ways in which novels unfold the relationship between the individual and society that *The Domain of the Novel* makes a significant contribution to the two lines of thinking on characterization that have long been at the centre of novel theory. The first is the tradition that treats the character of the realistic novel as a site for taxonomizing society – the tradition that began with the 19th-century Russian critics such as Vissarion Belinsky and Nikolay Dobrolyubov and that received its most sophisticated articulation in Georgi Lukacs's concept of the 'typical character'. Second, *The Domain of the Novel* engages in a sustained way with the tension that Nancy Armstrong put at the heart of liberal humanistic characterization – on the one hand, pure individuality that will not hesitate to confront established social systems and, on the other, the obligation that each individual has to restrain her individuality in order not to impinge on the rights of other individuals.⁴ Indeed, in the last lecture, Kaul breaks the vicious cycle by which the individual is granted untrammelled freedom only in order to be incorporated in the social system with brilliant readings of three American novels where characters whose inner lives are ideologically constituted are ejected by the shock of experience into what Jacques Ranciere, writing with specific reference to literature, would call the 'political'.⁵

Although *The Domain of the Novel* focusses overwhelmingly on the two modern entities that the novel brought into narrative – on the one hand a densely detailed social domain that replicated the structural limits of everyday life, and on the other hand the lifelike individual the richness of whose inner life was balanced by loss of stature granted to the epic hero – A. N. Kaul is remarkably sensitive to the novel's self-consciousness about what it has lost in the process of becoming itself. *The Domain of the Novel* begins with an invocation of Fielding's famous definition, in the 'Preface' to *Joseph Andrews*, of the new form he was pioneering. What he was offering, Fielding wrote, was 'a comic, epic poem in prose'.⁶ The critical terms here are, as Kaul well knew, 'comic' and 'prose'. Nevertheless, he chooses to uncover first a continued longing within the 19th-century novel for possibilities that disappeared with the form that it was displacing. The 'epic' that Fielding refuses to let go erupts everywhere in *Middlemarch*, written more than 130 years after *Joseph Andrew*, and the 'epic deeds', 'epic life', 'epic destiny' that Eliot constantly invokes may, as Kaul insightfully argues, be read as signposting a metatextual comment on the novel's incapacity for sustaining 'aspiration to fundamental world alteration' (*Domain* 23, 24).

Kaul's focus, thirty years ago, on the epic and on the long shadow of loss that it cast on some to the greatest novels of the 19th century turns out to be prescient. Basing themselves on the contrast that Hegel makes in *Aesthetics* (Vol. 1), between, on the one hand, the untrammelled scope of individual action in the 'heroic age' of epics and, on the other, 'the world of prose and everyday' where the individual's action is mediated by the 'social establishment' – its laws, institutions and social conventions – several recent scholars on novel theory have drawn attention precisely to *Middlemarch* as what Ginsburg and Nandrea have called 'the perfect illustration of Hegel's prose of the world'.[7]

Yet what Hegel and, it is good to remember, Fielding too called prose turned out to be characterized by a strong ambiguity. On the one hand, the impediment, as we have seen, of hardened social institutions forced it to adapt to what Max Weber called 'the rationalization of modern life', 'a process that begins in the economy and in the administration, but ultimately pervades the sphere of free time, private life, entertainment, feelings'. On the other hand, it becomes the basis of what Franco Moretti called, in an essay which Professor Kaul would have loved for its intelligence and clarity, 'a new analytical-impersonal style – which makes possible in its turn a new type of description where the world is observed with more precision and impartiality'.[8] We could argue, thus, that the constriction of the individual in the prosaic world of the novel was inseparable from a new style capable of orchestrating an unlimited range of details to create an internally consistent and plausible social world that would become the vital enabling condition for the new type of narrative called the novel. 'What Fielding had that Defoe lacked', Catherine Gallagher writes, marking the final step that needed to be taken for the emergence of the novel in England, 'was a special way of shaping knowledge through the fabrication of particulars'.[9]

The key word here is 'knowledge'. Gallagher's own brilliant work on the novel, sustained over several years, uncovers the whole complex set of factors by which the simulation of a densely detailed social world and of lifelike individuals came to be understood as a special kind of fictional knowledge by a historically constituted readership trained in the conditional investment of belief. Balzac's insistence that novelists had a better grasp than other writers over the 'archaeology of social furniture', Jacques Ranciere's idea of the 'silent speech' that novels borrowed from paintings to make an object speak 'exhibit signs written on [its] body', 'marks directly imparted by . . . history', Michael McKeon's assertion that the rise of the novel was inseparable from the widespread acceptance of verisimilitude as 'a form of truth', all testify that through the course of the 19th century, novels had become accepted sources of social knowledge.[10]

The conviction that novels are the bearers of a special kind of social knowledge lies at the heart of *The Domain of the Novel*. The constricting social world of *Middlemarch* may thwart Lydgate's world-altering ambitions, but the networks of intrigue; aspirations scientific, social and political; landscapes and habitations that weave and interweave to form a whole world that Eliot calls 'A Study of Provincial Life' has also been described by a famous historian, Kaul reports, with great appreciation, as 'the finest picture he knew of England at the time of the Reform Bill' (p. 25). Similarly, Eliot may compare Dorothea to a 'fine quotation from the bible, – or from one of our older poets', lost in the columns of 'today's newspaper',[11] but for Kaul – newspapers, and indeed, the prose of the world generally – emblematize the value of novels in ways that a quotation from the Bible or John Donne never could. Not only *Middlemarch* but *Vanity Fair* and *Tom Jones* as well are, Kaul writes, 'the newspapers of a century or an epoch, the representation of the structure of a whole society in its historical evolution' (p. 30).

Yet, of course, the value of novels are not exhausted by their straightforward documentation of the past. Rather, Kaul is interested in that special quality in novels that distinguished them from, as Gallagher observed, both 'fact and deception'[12] and specifically in the effects produced by the license realistic novels have to creatively improvise within the limits of the 'plausible'. In his first lecture, Kaul focuses on the ways in which 18th- and 19th-century English novelists imagined and improvised within the protocols of realism the relationship between a social world that readers recognized and the imagined lives of characters. Indeed, it is important for him to distinguish his way of thinking from that of critics who, in their anxiety to historicize, lose sight of the novel's ability to conjure imagined individuals who are unique yet socially constituted. Barbara Hardy may be right, Kaul argues, in describing Thackeray as 'a great accumulator of social symbols of class and money', but her description 'is also totally inadequate, totally dependent on external symbolization, and totally unaware of the subtle ways in which he fuses the individual with the social, the inner with the outer, the psychological with the sociological' (p. 32).

By locating the value of novels in their depiction of what Georgi Lukacs called 'the changeful texture of the external and internal, the great and little moments that make up life',[13] Kaul is able to connect the slightest movement in the inner life of a character to fault lines not just in intermediary institutions like marriage or family but in the structure of society itself. In this, Kaul is clearly following a tradition in literary criticism that began with Vissarion Belinsky and Nikolay Dobrolyubov – the so-called

Russian Democratic critics – and culminated in Georgi Lukacs's *Studies in European Realism*. Kaul acknowledges his sympathy with this tradition of criticism at several points of *The Domain of the Novel*, but he also touches on an element that often enters into the ways novels negotiate the relationship between the social and the personal and that features in the work, not so much of Lukacs as of his ideological successor Fredric Jameson.

The problem that Jameson discusses in his seminal 'Experiments of Time' is the place of moral qualities like good, evil, virtue, vice in the realist novels of the 19th century. These qualities, Jameson argues, belong to a transcendent 'meta social' realm. As such they 'cast an unsettling doubt over the "ontological assurances" of realism'. Jameson's argument that realism should logically be hostile to transcendental values is carried forward by Jacques Ranciere in a response to Sartre's charge that Flaubert's writing was 'petrified'. On the contrary, Ranciere argues, Flaubert took the realist project to its logical conclusion by achieving the moral 'indifference' of 'an archaeologist or geologist who gets mute witnesses of common history to speak'.

As Jameson himself notes, however, English realists, unlike Flaubert and his successors, held on to the transcendental, ethical and, in Barthes's sense of the term, 'meaning' producing dimension of fiction. More specifically, Jameson argues that the ethical element was not so much marginalized in English fiction as modulated and made to work within the bounds of a 'realistic and empirical world'.[14]

Kaul, too, notes the presence of 'meta social' values in realist novels to come out of England: the 'all capitalised HUMAN NATURE' in Fielding, 'Pride' which, as Dickens wrote in his 'Preface' to the novel, was going to be the theme of *Dombey and Son* and, most obviously, Vanity which is encoded in the very title of *Vanity Fair*. Like – and, let it be noted, before – Jameson, Kaul sees these trans social values as the residue of 'the older modes of thought as well as older modes and subjects of literature'. Anyone who has studied with Professor Kaul will testify that his contempt for the moralized characters of Victorian novels matched Jameson's acerbic: 'nor have they gone all the way toward those allegories in which nameless figures bear their designations on their backs in the form of signs (I am Envy, I am Complacency), but we are close'.[15] Kaul, however, also draws attention to the 'internal struggles' within 19th-century novels as they go about redefining these 'traditional moral-universal categories – human nature, pride, vanity . . . in terms of contemporary, material realities' (p. 33). For Kaul the most interesting result of this 'internal struggle' is the radical ambiguity that it introduces in the figure who acts as the narrator of *Vanity Fair*. Anticipating a configuration that would resonate powerfully with the modern sensibility, Thackeray combines the functions of priest and clown in the figure of this narrator. Kaul's interest in the figure of the clown masquerading as a priest points to a potentially powerful line of argument on how the 'meta social' ethical impulse unfolded in 19th-century English novels generally, that *The Domain of the Novel* doesn't fully develop. But we, who have studied with A. N. Kaul, remember the importance that he gave to irony – that is to the tone of the clown rather than the preacher – in his lectures on the English novel. It was for him the one mode in which 19th-century English novelists had greater mastery over their counterparts in France and Russia. I imagine him now speaking to Fredric Jameson in this domain of ideas where distance and even death have no power to impede:

> It is not around the play of vice or virtue but rather around the irony that geminates in the gap between love and class allegiance, between vocation and the desire for a comfortable life that English novels organize, what you're calling their 'meta social' ethical meaning.

More than in older types of ethical categories like 'pride' or 'vanity', Kaul is interested in the contemporary concept of 'ideology' and the ways in which it shapes characters. Indeed, he devotes the whole of his third lecture to engaging with this problem and I will turn in the last part of this Introduction to the powerful criticism he mounts against the ideological determinism that underlay the work of Americanists such as Sacvan Bercovitch and Myra Jehlen.

But before he turns to ideology, Kaul probes the novel's reconstitution of both the individual and the social as they are brought into an inexorable relationship with an entity that is larger than both. In his lecture 'Nationality and the Novel' (Chapter 2), Kaul's canvas expands dramatically. Indeed, he moves into a terrain that would today be instantly recognized as the terrain of world literature. What is more, as he works his way through the different ways in which novels in England, Russia, America and India configured their relationship with the idea of nationhood, Kaul outlines paradigms that continue to drive the thinking on the relationship between the novel and nationalism to this day.

For Kaul, the English novel offers the simplest and least interesting illustration of how a sense of the nation was both produced and disseminated by the novel. Specifically, drawing on a central idea in Hippolyte Taine's writing – elaborated endlessly by subsequent generations of historians and sociologists – Kaul argues that the English novel replicated the process of constant social amelioration that both preserved England from the revolutionary upheavals that swept across Europe and produced the internal social integration critical for England's self-definition as a nation. English novels, Kaul argues, were self-consciously oriented to perpetuating this integration:

horizontally across the country's regional variations in *Tom Jones*, vertically across class in *Vanity Fair*, and if Jane Austen's eponymous heroine is ideologically oriented towards distinguishing herself from mere yeomen, the whole purpose of *Emma* is to cure her of her snobbery.

Two important books – James Buzard's *Disorienting Fiction* (2005) and John Plotz's *Portable Property* (2008) – that came out after Professor Kaul's lectures confirmed his sense that the English novel's preoccupation with English national culture made these novels insular and inward looking at a time when, paradoxically, Britain itself was leading the drive towards internationalization. In *Disorienting Fiction*, Buzard comments on the strange reluctance of the English novel, 'the preeminent genre of nineteenth century', to engage with colonialism, 'the preeminent fact about Europe during this period'. Buzard attributes this orientation to the 'very expansion of colonial holdings and international entanglements' and to the anxiety that it caused about 'where and what Britishness or Englishness might be'. The British novelist, therefore, increasingly took recourse to what Mary Louise Pratt might have called 'metropolitan autoethnography': 'the *recovery*', as Buzard puts it 'of an Anglocentric cultural identity during a phase of intensive, imperial, industrial and commercial expansion' (italics in original). In a subsequent study, Plotz shows that novels (together with English objects and rituals) served Victorian administrators, merchants and other professionals working in colonies as the means of preserving intact their Englishness threatened from all sides by the contaminants of a surrounding native culture.[16]

In a move whose implications are continuing to play out productively to this day, Kaul contrasts the inward looking homogenizing impulse that national consciousness brought to English novels with the broader, more varied and conflicted ways in which novels from Russia, India and America negotiated the experience of what Kaul in a wonderfully balanced phrase calls 'belated nationality'. For Kaul, the critical difference between the English novel and its counterparts in Russia, India and America was that the latter engaged *simultaneously* with the internal social dynamics of their own countries and the larger processes of modernization that were sweeping across the world. For novels coming out of these countries, he writes:

> the Western model was already there as a compelling, inescapable, *external* point of reference or conflicting presence. So was the natio and the native, not easily harmonizable with the imported model of nationality but often resistant, like a polar opposite, leading to a debate or a dialectic rather than an easy cohesion between the two, the native both resisting and yet accepting the Western nationalist imagination.

(p. 42)

For Kaul, the 'discourse, both political and literary' that came out of this tension is 'more complex . . . richer, more radical in some ways, more contentious and problematic, than the internally self-defining, homogenizing discourse of western European nationalism' (p. 42). Yet, although he brings together novels from Russia, America and India as a group formed in some significant way by the experience of 'belated nationality', Kaul carefully distinguishes between the ways that the Russian, Indian and American novels negotiated their own sense of nationhood. Of the three, probably the Russian novel derived the maximum energy from the experience of Russia's belated nationhood, although it was a tortured, self-lacerating energy that gave so many 19th-century novels that dark, brooding, peculiarly modern mood.

For Kaul, as for so many scholars of Russian novels, Russia's national consciousness became riven with conflicts ever since Peter the Great decided to Europeanize a nation built on czarism, the Russian Orthodox Church, serf labour and large landed estates. If Kaul had had the benefit of research published after he delivered these lectures, he would have given even greater significance to the corrosive relationship between the sensibilities of a Westernized Russian elite and the workings of a socio-economic system that was nowhere near acquiring the productive efficiency of Europe. Always a materialist, he would have been delighted to discover that the tension so central to his reading of Russian novels reached down to what William Mills Todd has called the 'institutional conditions' in which those novels were produced. On the one hand, publishing as a business was underdeveloped in comparison to Europe: characterized by what Todd has called 'minimally professionalised authorship, uncertain readership, precarious publishing networks through the periodical press'. On the other hand, the classic Russian novels of the 1840s, many of which Kaul discusses, 'were written for a small elite audience that could be counted on to recognize the echoes of Byron, Rousseau, Scott, Sterne and other European writers but that knew little Russian fiction'.[17] This tension between European ideas and an underdeveloped economy produced what Kaul, quoting Dobrolyubov, called 'our native, national type' (p. 44). Thus, Pushkin's Onegin, Lermontov's Pechorin and Goncharov's Oblomov may be highly educated and gifted individuals but caught between a superficially Westernized elite and the stagnation of traditional Russia they are trapped in an irresolvable deadlock. The result is, as Kaul puts it with reference to Eugene Onegin, 'a negative critique of negative values leading, not to a positive resolution, but to a question mark: What is the future of Russia as a nation? What does the Western intrusion portend? In novelistic terms: Who or what is Onegin?'

The answer is, to follow Kaul in quoting from Onegin, 'Just an apparition / a showdown, null and meaningless', 'a Muscovite in [Childe] Harold's dress / a modish second-hand edition' (p. 45).

Kaul manages here, as he did so often in his lectures and his books, to put his finger on that exact brilliantly defined configuration that captures not only that unresolvable sense of anxiety and rootlessness that would be encoded in so many subsequent characters, but also of the dark, peculiarly modern mood that pervades some of Russia's greatest novels. Not even God would have managed to track the line that led through many mutations from Onegin to Raskolnikov or have paused to reflect on the suffocating atmosphere with which Dostoevsky envelops the city that Peter the Great had built to integrate Russia to European modernity, in a lecture which had America and India as well on its agenda. But Pushkin's description of Onegin as 'Just an apparition / a showdown, null and meaningless', 'a Muscovite in [Childe] Harold's dress / a modish second-hand edition', does capture what Marshall Berman called (in a phrase that lacks the nuance and balance of Kaul's 'belated nationality') 'the modernism of underdevelopment'. Unlike the progressive, linear sense of history that underlay the European novel and that produced, among other things, the *bildungsroman*, the 'modernism of underdevelopment' that Berman associates with the Russian novel 'turns in on itself and tortures itself for its inability to singlehandedly make history . . . and whips itself into frenzies of self-loathing, and preserves itself only through vast reserves of self- irony'.[18]

Kaul's task becomes much more complicated as he moves from Russia to India, above all because the variables that mediate the relationship between India's belated nationality and the early Indian novel increase dramatically. The range of languages used in vernacular Indian novels – to take just one example – suggests the difficulties involved in the enterprise on which Kaul embarks. Adding to these difficulties is Kaul's decision to veer away from what he calls 'the most interesting material for the present context' (p. 51) – vernacular novels written through the latter half of the 19th century – on the grounds that he does not have the professional competence to do scholarly work in India's regional languages. Despite these limitations – despite falling back on one English language novelist, R.K. Narayan, and juxtaposing his fiction briefly with the work of Salman Rushdie and writers who followed him – Kaul still manages to stimulate our thinking on the ways in which novels in India negotiated their belated experience of nationhood along two interesting directions.

First, Kaul links Narayan's novels to a much more general preoccupation which he believed, on the basis of his lifelong familiarity (distinct, as he always insisted, from professional competence) with novels written in at least two regional languages, to be characteristic of *any* work of imaginative literature that came out of the experience of India's belated sense of nationhood. This is the 'theme of all modern history, society, politics, and directly or indirectly, overtly or implicitly, all modern Indian literature as well – the theme of the East and the West'. Indeed Kaul argues, that 'the *comic* confusion of the native and the foreign' played out in Narayan's novels embodies what Graham Greene called, with reference to one of Narayan's novels, 'a whole national condition' (p. 52).

'[T]he comic confusion of the native and foreign' is exactly what I'd discovered to be at the heart of *Hootum Pyanchar Naksha* (1861) – a book about city life in Calcutta in the middle of the 19th century on which I've written two recent essays. During the course of research for those essays, I'd had the good fortune to read the absolutely brilliant work of historians like Ranajit Guha, Sudipta Kaviraj and Dipesh Chakrabarty: work that probed with precision the stakes involved as the claims of the 'west and the east' jostled each other at every conceivable level of life in 19th-century Bengal: in its unfolding intimate relationships, the conduct of its festivals, the representation of its gods and goddesses and, above all, its experience of time. I imagine Professor Kaul now, hovering around the pages of this book, turning with increasing interest to *Provincializing Europe* (2000) or *The Invention of Private Life* (2015) and asking himself why he should not brush up his Urdu and Hindi and begin exploring how his ideas about the comic confusion of the native and foreign would mutate as he moved back to the 19th century where his professional expertise would enable him to move effortlessly between continents and when, in India, the chaotic intermixtures of the east and west were at their most turbulent.

Kaul's comments on the Indian novel stimulates a second line of thinking that has to do not so much with the complications caused by India's belated sense of its nationality as with the alacrity with which the idea of nationhood was given up by the generation of novelists who followed Narayan. Malgudi, the small town in which almost all of Narayan's stories are set, is bound by what Kaul, in a detailed introductory discussion on theories of nationalism, calls 'the hard facts' of nationhood: matters of economic, political and administrative organization (p. 37–8). It may be described in Narayan's impeccable English and bear the marks of British colonial rule at many levels, but it is still a small Indian town with limited resources that will allow its inhabitants few opportunities for mobility.

In contrast to Narayan, whose stories are shaped entirely by the closely observed details of the small town, several writers who followed Rushdie's spectacular internationalization of the Indian novel begin with the assumption that in a globalized world, no place can be called home. When in 'The Lady from Lucknow', Bharati Mukherjee writes 'The traveller feels at home everywhere, because she is never at home anywhere', she announces, Kaul argues, 'the end of nationality' (p. 54).

The transnational canvas of writers like Salman Rushdie and so many others was consistent with the increasing pressure mounted on the concept of nation-states by major contemporary political theorists, some of whom Kaul discusses at the beginning of his lecture. Kaul, on the other hand, links 'the end of nationality' in the Indian English novel with the social location of writers who came to dominate it in the 1980s and 1990s. Upper class, often expatriates 'with frequent and easy access across national borders', these writers refused to remain tied down to any constricting idea of nationhood. For Kaul, on the other hand, the breach between the novel and nationality that Rushdie and his successors affected in the Indian novel also points to the increasing gap between the novelist and the 'natio', that is, 'the place where one is born, a micro-entity, family, domicile, local community, the condition of belonging' (p. 37). In this sense the transnational direction that the Indian English novel takes during the last decades of the 20th century diffuses the extremely productive tension that Kaul had associated with the relationship between novels and the experience of 'belated nationality'. This is what accounts for that tone of unease with which Kaul ends the lecture on the novel and nationality.

> Does this then signal the end of nationality as a literary theme or does this apply only to the Indian novelists who write in English? All I can say by way of conclusion is that I find it rather astonishing that, in a gymnastic feat of high calibre, the Indian novel in English should, in the space of one generation, have moved from the struggle to define the national condition to the freewheeling exposition of what Zbigniew Brzezinski, National Security Advisor to President Jimmy Carter, called 'a new planetary consciousness'.
>
> (p. 55)

As Kaul moves to the American novel, his thoughts on novels and 'belated nationalities' acquire a resonance that is more far reaching than anything he'd said in relation to the Russian or the Indian novel. This is not surprising, of course, since A. N. Kaul has long been one of the world's leading scholars on 19th-century American literature. Thus, Kaul uses that unique feature of America's sense of nationhood – the frontier – to engage with problems of novelistic form, with cutting edge ideology critique that was reshaping his beloved American novels in ways he disliked and, above all, with the great philosophical questions about literature itself – its status as a source of knowledge and its capacity or incapacity to make a difference to the social organization of the real world.

What distinguished America from Russia and India was that, unlike the latter, it had no past since, as Kaul points out sarcastically, 'native Indians and bison did not count' (p. 46). For this reason, there were no pre-existing cultural values or political institutions that could bring America's sense of its nationality into conflict with ideas and structures that had developed in Europe. Rather, the conflict was articulated in relation to America's vison of the future: 'the repudiation of Europe or the Old World on the one hand', as Kaul puts it, 'and, on the other, defining America or the New World as "the open frontier of boundless possibility"'. Indeed, if there is, to continue quoting Kaul, 'one national archetypal character that stands at the pole from the types of European nationality it would be [the] *figure poised on the frontier*' (p. 47, italics in original).

The frontiersman, in fact, embodies a dynamic that was to prove crucial to the American novel at multiple levels. Suffocated by the hardening of structures in the new world settlements that increasingly replicate the social and political processes of Europe, the frontiersman moves away to clear the wilderness. But as the wilderness that he has cleared becomes the site of a fresh settlement, he finds himself compelled to light out again deeper into uncharted territory. The frontiersman, therefore, performs two functions that for Kaul prove to be critical for the American novel at the level of both form and content. First, he pushes the American novel into a terrain that is free of the structured social world that underpins the European novel. That is, he pushes the novel in the direction of the romance – the form from which the novel had gradually separated through the course of the 18th century as it began to increasingly embed itself in the familiar, more or less predictable processes of a fully formed social domain. At the same time unlike the traditional romance, the 19th-century American novel does not assume a pre-social world. Rather, if Natty Bumppo, Hester Prynne or Huckleberry Finn are 'poised on the frontier', it is because of their 'critical relation to establishment values such as marriage, family, property *and*, in the American context, *racism*' (p. 47, italics in original).

The link that Kaul makes between America's 'belated nationality' and a *new* form of romance is important and deserves elaboration. Here it is crucial to distinguish the traditional romance – both ancient and contemporary – that is innocent of the social domain from the way Kaul conceptualizes the American novel. Thus, far from being (in Clara Reeves's classic definition) 'the heroic fable which treats of fabulous persons and things . . . in lofty and elevated language . . . and describes what never happened or is likely to happen', the American Romance does not disregard or run away from, but engages with realism's presentation of the social domain when we take into account the potential for 'conservatism and anti-politicality' that Fredric Jameson associates with that presentation:

> An ontological realism absolutely committed to the density and solidity of what is – whether in the realm of psychology and feelings,

institutions, objects or space – cannot but be threatened in the very nature of the form by any suggestion that things are changeable and not ontologically immutable: the very choice of the form is itself a professional endorsement of status quo.[19]

For Kaul, the new Romance form necessary to accommodate the frontiersman becomes a way of breaking realism's stranglehold over the real. It is, he says,

> a mode of writing which involves the strategy of breaking away from reality and realism in order to subject them – that is, both 19th century socio-historical reality and its appropriate socio-historical mode of representation – to a critique from alien and alienating points of view or vantage.

(p. 66–7)

As we shall see, what Kaul stakes with this proposition is nothing less than the nature of the political work that novels do. But in order to understand the magnitude and urgency of Kaul's claim, we first have to turn to his third and, in many ways, his most complex lecture, where he outlines with great erudition and sophistication a certain way of conceptualizing the relationship between the outer and the inner, society and the individual, that wielded great influence in American Studies from the last decades of the 20th century.

'Ideology and the Novel' (Chapter 3) begins with a sustained and critical engagement with the thought of Louis Althusser. Kaul tracks back the genealogy of Althusser's thought to Karl Marx and Antonio Gramsci; he uncovers the many, often contradictory, ways in which Althusser himself deployed the term; and he rewrites Althusser's 'Ideological State Apparatuses' as 'institutional matrices of ideology' since institutions 'such as Family, Education, Church, Religion can hardly be called State Apparatuses' (p. 63). And although he will confront head on the more deterministic strands of Althusser's thought as it plays out in the literary criticism of scholars like Sacvan Bercovitch and Myra Jehlen, what Kaul takes back from Althusser is his contribution towards our understanding of the nature of domination.

For Kaul, the sources of ideological domination are myriad but always external. There are the more obvious, easily discernible sources of ideological dissemination such as the family, educational and religious institutions but, beyond these, 'a whole range of cultural practices and signifying systems'. More than the sources of ideology, though, Kaul is interested in what ideology does to the internal domain of consciousness. The penetration of ideology within consciousness is so deep that

> that it is no longer a matter of ideas or ideas only, but something deeper than ideas, something that shapes and structures our ideas as well as our values, our feelings, our very perceptions, from even sensory perceptions to the perceptions of signs including linguistic signs. Ideology, one may thus say, is like the air which surrounds us on all sides, which we breathe constantly but which we ordinarily never notice – unless suffocated!
>
> (p. 63)

Clearly, Kaul has a deep interest in the power of ideology to constitute the subject. Indeed, he is convinced that several 19th-century novelists – Thackeray in England, Melville, Hawthorne and Twain in America – deserve to be called 'pre-Althusser Althusserians' (p. 63) because their understanding of the relationship between ideology and subjectivity was no less sophisticated than their late 20th-century critics.

But for Kaul, the pervasiveness of ideology does not engulf the novel form itself. On the contrary, he confronts critics like Bercovitch and Jehlen precisely because they conceptualize the novel as so completely constituted by ideology that every element in its form or content becomes yet another conduit by which ideology enters the consciousness of the reader to do its subtle work. Kaul, as we have already noted, contests this assertion at the level of form, arguing that the Romance is configured to allow for a space, which is outside established society, and therefore outside all pervasive influence of ideology. Moreover, while Kaul is always alert to workings of ideology in the deepest layers of the consciousness of characters who inhabit American novels, he is even more interested in that moment of infraction when a character, working within the constraints of a socially constituted reality, is confronted with what Kaul calls an unprecedented experience. Working from within the Marxist tradition, Kaul associates 'experience' with what the Marx of *The German Ideology* called 'altered circumstances' in contradistinction to 'theoretical deductions', and what E.P. Thompson more than a century later described as crises: 'crises of subsistence, trench warfare, unemployment, inflation, genocide' (p. 64).

Kaul, it should be clear, does not locate 'experience' in some mystical or transcendental realm that frees the subject from the compulsions of the social world. Instead, 'experience', in Kaul's sense, *reconfigures* the social so that the individual is able to see it with new eyes. Kaul demonstrates how this happens with scintillating readings of three classic American novels. If

I were to pick one paragraph that sums up the argument he makes in the last pages of this book, it would be the following:

> I will only refer to one romance feature of these novels, not the continuous fabric of a setting, but the disjunction of settings – between the raft on the river and the slave-owning society on the shore in *Huckleberry Finn*, or the Calvinist settlement and the wilderness, the wild forest, in *The Scarlet Letter* – which I see as the explorations of alternative social possibilities. And I mean it and will be prepared to defend it, right now by quoting authority: as an exploration of alternative social possibilities, the creation, in Marx's phrase, of 'altered circumstances', or, as Brecht, the leading theoretician of the 'epic theatre' or the 'dialectical theatre' and himself immersed in Marxist thought, puts it, 'experiments' to test social truths, to strive 'towards an entirely new social function'.
>
> (p. 67)

This passage highlights once again what anyone who has studied with A. N. Kaul already knows: that he combined his good humour and an impossibly relaxed mode of presentation with ideas of great complexity. Here he links a formal feature of the romance, the 'disruption of setting' that it was always capable of effecting and the subjective experience of 'altered circumstances', to something much larger – a reconfiguration of the world as it has been understood. In this he reinforces a conviction that made his classes a life-changing experience for so many of us: the conviction that literature mattered because it always had the capacity to make us look at the world with new eyes.

I imagine him now walking out of what was perhaps one of the last lectures of his life and then out of this book with the sad eyes of Ricardo Reis: detached from a world that he no longer inhabits but troubled by the sense that the more deterministic strains of Althusser's thinking have got an even stronger grip on novel theory, and that the discursive depth and formal innovativeness that he (Kaul) celebrated in 19th-century novels are now understood as precisely the resources that the novel needed to do the work of turning, as Nancy Armstrong put it in a 2006 book, 'the individual's natural excess into the cultural wisdom of the citizen subject'.[20]

I do want to tell Professor Kaul, however, before I reach the end of this Introduction and say goodbye to him again, that he is not without allies even in a world that is increasingly sceptical if not hopeless about the power of literature to think the unthinkable. I want to invoke, in this marvellous world of letters where distance or even death are not barriers for the meeting of minds, the work of a man who, by a strange and exhilarating irony, turns out to be Louis Althusser's most brilliant student and onetime collaborator. Unlike his teacher, Jacques Ranciere is interested not in the incorporating trajectory of ideology but in that process of visiblization and reconfiguration that he calls 'politics'. The constituency most capable of participating in politics, as Ranciere understands it, coincides precisely with the folk who, in Kaul's account, enter the American novel, indeed the novel form as such: 'protagonists of low, even at times marginal, rank, engaged in living ordinary lives in commonplace pursuits of the commonest of commonplace goals' (p. 22). Politics is what occurs, Ranciere writes, when

> those men and women who don't have the time to do anything other than their work, take time that they don't have to prove that they are indeed speaking beings, participating in a shared world and not indeed furious or suffering animals. This distribution and this redistribution of space and time, place and identity, speech and noise, the visible and invisible, form what I call the distribution of the perceptible. Political activity reconfigures the distribution of the perceptible. It introduces new objects and new subjects onto the common stage. It makes visible what was invisible, it makes audible as speaking beings those who were previously heard only as noisy animals.[21]

The 'political' breaks through the stranglehold of ideology again and again in the novels that Professor Kaul discusses in these lectures, and I can do no better than conclude with a powerful political statement he makes in relation to his favourite novel, *The Scarlet Letter*, in what appears as the last lecture in this book

> And without going into details I think this comes across if we see *The Scarlet Letter* not merely as a story about the Puritans, but if we see it, number one, as Hester's tragedy played against the grain of the world that the Puritans wished established; number two, if we try to examine the meaning of Hester's tragic challenge; number three, if we try to examine the meaning of Hester's tragic illumination which makes her rise above her world at one point and judge it, judge it not in its own terms but in larger terms, [from the] perspectives maybe of the future... [we would have to conclude] as I suggested – 'As a first step, the whole system of society is to be torn down, and built up anew'. If put in discursive prose I think this is what Hawthorne would be saying in *The Scarlet Letter*.

(p. 88–9)

Notes

1 Catherine Gallagher, 'The Rise of Fictionality', in *The Novel: History, Geography and Culture*, ed. Franco Moretti, Vol. 1 (Princeton: Princeton University Press, 2006), pp. 336–63, 361.

2 Guido Mazzoni, *Theory of the Novel*, trans. Zakia Hanafi (Cambridge: Harvard University Press, 2017), p. 21. See also Thomas Pavel, 'The Novel in Search of Itself: A Historical Morphology', in *The Novel: History, Forms and Themes*, ed. Franco Moretti, Vol. 2 (Princeton: Princeton University Press, 2006), pp. 3–32.

3 See Pavel, 'The Novel in Search of Itself', p. 17 and Mazzoni, *Theory of the Novel*, p. 129.

4 See Nancy Armstrong, *How Novels Think: The Limits of Individualism from 1719–1900* (New York: Columbia University Press, 2005), esp. pp. 48–52.

5 Jacques Ranciere, 'The Politics of Literature', in *The Politics of Literature*, trans. Julie Rose (Cambridge: The Polity Press, 2011), pp. 3–31.

6 Quoted in A. N. Kaul, *The Domain of the Novel* (New Delhi: Routledge & Kegan Paul, 2021), p. 21 All subsequent quotations are from this edition and page numbers appear after quoted passages in parentheses.

7 G.W.F. Hegel, *Aesthetics, Lectures on Fine Arts*, trans. T.M. Knox (Oxford: Clarendon Press, 1975), p. 149 and Michal Ginsburg and Lorri Nandrea, 'The Prose of the World', in *Novel*, ed. Franco Moretti, Vol. 2, p. 248.

8 In Franco Moretti, 'Serious Century', in *Novel*, ed. Franco Moretti, Vol. 1, p. 376, and Webber quoted in 381.

9 Gallagher, 'Fictionality', 344.

10 See Catherine Gallagher, *Nobody's Story: The Vanishing Acts of Women Writers in the Marketplace, 1670–1820* (Berkeley, CA: University of California Press, 1994), Ranciere, 'Politics', p. 22, Jacques Ranciere, *The Future of the Image* (New Delhi: Navayana, 2010), p. 13, Michael McKeon, *The Origins of the English Novel: 1600–1740* (Baltimore: The Johns Hopkins University Press, 1987).

11 George Eliot, *Middlemarch* (1872) (London: W.W. Norton & Co., 2000), p. 5.

12 Gallagher, 'Fictionality', p. 338.

13 Georgi Lukacs, *Studies in European Realism*, trans. Edith Bone (London: The Merlin Press, 1978), p. 153.

14 Fredric Jameson, *The Experiments of Time*, p. 110, *Novel*, ed. Franco Moretti, Vol. 1.

15 Jameson, 'Experiments', p. 110.

16 James Buzard, *Disorienting Fiction,* pp. 43, 51 and 107, and Unsigned, 'The Progress of Fiction', *Westminster Review* LX, October 1853, p. 343.

17 William Mills Todd, 'The Ruse of the Russian Novel', in *Novel*, ed. Moretti, Vol. 1, p. 413.

18 Marshall Berman, *All that is Solid Melts in the Air* (London: Penguin Books, 1982), p. 232.

19 Clara Reeves, quoted in Mazzoni, *Theory of Novel*, p. 83 and Jameson, 'Experiments', p. 113.

20 Armstrong, *How Novels Think,* p. 55.

21 Ranciere, 'Politics', p. 4.

1 'A new province of writing'

I am grateful to Sri Venkateswara College, the English Department, and especially Pradip, Anwer and Sambudha, for inviting me to give these lectures on the novel.

Almost every literate person today, if he or she reads anything apart from newspapers, reads novels. Worse, many literate persons also either write novels or harbour secret thoughts of writing them. The general idea seems to be that if you have lived a life you can write at least one story, preferably your own. One man/woman, one vote; one life, one novel!

Fiction is the most democratic, not to say narcissistic, of literary genres, also anarchistic inasmuch as no kind of discipline seems to be called for, no apprenticeship or training, no rules of the game. It is hardly a literary genre any longer but, as an American might put it, a jungle out there, which literary jungle has hosted, on top of itself, a parasitical critical jungle of its own.

This being so, it would be not only pretentious but futile to attempt anything like mapping the *Domain* of the novel. My purpose in these lectures is rather to go back in time to the earliest novelists's and focus on a handful of old and old-fashioned novels in order to see where and how it all began, starting out in each case with these novelists' own demarcation or definition of their domain, the territory they thought they were staking out for themselves, and the signposts they were hanging out for their own and future times. I shall begin with their definitions and understanding but our understanding will include but also, naturally, go beyond those definitions and, in the present case, this broader understanding will be based on (a) reading the novels together, synchronically, as it were, and (b) more important, focussing on the domain of the novel in and through the surrounding interactive domains of history, society and politics.

I would like to make two further prefatory points. One, when I say old and old-fashioned, I mean the 18th and early 19th centuries when the novel first emerged in Europe, to my way of thinking, as a part of the general process of overhauling the older formations of life as well as the old forms of literature. Second, if there is any single thesis running through these lectures, it is a simple one: namely, that the domain of the novel is, and was from the outset, an internally conflicted, a dialogical or dialectical domain – three fashionable words all at once! – fascinating to me not because of the polarities themselves but the way in which various novelists try to manage or resolve these polarities.

My lecture today will focus largely on some well-known English novels. The second lecture, under the rubric of 'Nationality and the Novel', will focus mainly on novels produced in a few countries which had what I term a sense of 'belated nationality' such as early 19th-century Russia and late 19th-century India. The focus of the third lecture will be on a few 19th-century American novels under the general rubric of 'Ideology and the Novel', which is in itself a concept that in a preliminary way bridges the polarities where the individual and the political, the psychological and the social, are identically one and the same.

The subject today being the English novel, the beginning point inevitably is Henry Fielding who, when he turned from stage comedies and farces to prose fiction, thought of himself as 'the founder of a new province of writing' (*Tom Jones*, Bk. 2, Ch. 1, 53), and, accordingly, considered it incumbent upon himself to define this new literary territory, which he did in his prefatory writings. Repetitiously and almost exclusively through the use of oxymorons, right at the outset, some of the polarities I spoke of a moment ago get expressed in contradictory meanings within Fielding's definitions of the novel, most famously in the definition 'a comic epic poem in prose' in the Preface to *Joseph Andrews* (Preface, 60), varied later in *Tom Jones* to such phrases as 'prosai-comi-epic writing' (Bk. 5, Ch. 1, 137) and a 'heroic, historical, prosaic poem' (Bk. 4, Ch. 1, 100). In *Tom Jones* he also defined his work as 'the narrative of plain matter of fact . . . a newspaper of many volumes' (Bk. 4, Ch. 1, 99–100), but at the same time ranked himself not with the journalists of the day but with *historians* of the same order as Homer and Milton. At other places he defined the novel as 'domestic history' or simply as the history, that is to say, the life or biography of one individual.

At one level, these linguistic contortions, these contradictions, can be seen as a neo-classical writer's awe of the ancient classics. The references to Homer and other writings of antiquity, including the lost Aristotelian treatise on Comedy, suggest the awareness of the Augustan writer that whatever may seem new will in fact turn out to be merely a new version of the old. But the matter is not so simple. And, indeed, there is a point here, for the domain of Fielding's novel can be seen as much the colonization of a new territory as the rehabilitation of an old literary terrain in various ways. The epic may be rejected but it gets reinscribed, or, in Shelley's dialectical imagery, may be eclipsed but is extinguished not (*Adonais*, Stanza 44).

This is, I think personally, the crux of Fielding's oxymoronic definition of the novel as a comic epic, and this, in varying ways, as I shall argue, suggests the doubleness between the comic and the epic, the individual and the socio-historical, private life and the epochal, which underlies a great many novels after Fielding up to our own day. But at present I would rather look only at one side of the argument and consider what is new and, indeed, revolutionary in Fielding's theory and practice as a novelist, namely his rejection of the epic. Not only his rejection of the epic protagonist of sublime-divine, mythological, or superhuman power and character, but more so, his epos as a fable involving not just his personal fortune but the whole history or destiny of some larger, collective entity – a tribe, a race, a community, a polis, a whole society or nation: the fall of Troy as in *The Iliad*, the founding of Rome as in Virgil's *Aeneid*, the story of a whole country as in *The Mahabharata*, the eternal destiny of all mankind as in Milton – 'In Adam's fall, we sinned all'.[1]

On the other hand, the installation of the Comic, in the sense of the commonplace, the ordinary, the topical, the matter of fact, protagonists of low, even at times marginal, rank, engaged in living ordinary lives in commonplace pursuits of the commonest of commonplace goals – marriage and the means of livelihood – in middle-class parlance, love and fortune, their fable involving no larger destiny than their own domestic, personal, private life, biographies of individuals rather than of history-making epic heroes.

All kinds of characters hitherto excluded from literature make their appearance centre-stage – Richardson's maidservant Pamela, Defoe's picara Moll Flanders, Fielding's own footman in *Joseph Andrews*, as well as the bastard Tom Jones. We remember how Edmund in *King Lear* had cried out, 'Now, gods, stand up for bastards!' (1.2.22), not too prematurely, I think, since by the time of *Tom Jones*, the gods of literature themselves were already standing up for bastards and rewarding bastards and other such common people, rewarding them with upward mobility through the fable of love and marriage – Richardson's maidservant Pamela ending as the wife of a country squire and Tom Jones winning not only the beautiful Sophia but also her estate as well as Squire Allworthy's estate called Paradise Hall.

The bastardy is, of course, to be understood socially rather than biologically, signifying the breaking in of the NEW man into the preserves of the older hierarchical classes. Glancing ahead, as we move into the 19th century, while these so-called common people in the so-called age of the common man become more respectable, more acceptable to society and literature, their mainstream fable remains essentially the story of love, marriage and private concerns. Indeed, 120 years after *Tom Jones*, George Eliot in *Middlemarch* raises again precisely this issue of the reduction of the novel's domain from the epic to the domestic, to mere stories of love and marriage, with a pointed reference in Chapter 15 to Fielding – a 'great historian, as he insisted on calling himself' (George Eliot's words, Bk. 2, Ch. 15, 96), and more specifically to Fielding's 'copious remarks and digressions' (Bk. 2, Ch. 15, 96) and especially the prefatory chapters in *Tom Jones* – in short, exactly the place where Fielding had elaborated his definition of the novel as comic epic.

George Eliot herself uses the word 'epic' constantly – 'epic deeds', 'epic life', 'epic destiny' – although in her case an equally appropriate word would be 'epochal' or 'epoch-making', that is, as the dictionary explains it, marking the beginning of an era in history, in science, in life. And it is this common element of the frustration of the epochal that made her combine two stories in *Middlemarch* as we have it today, the stories of her two protagonists, Dr. Lydgate and Dorothea Brooke, which, as we know, were originally conceived and partly written as separate works. So that one can read *Middlemarch* as a novel about novel-writing to the extent that its combined narrative engages *as a narrative*, the question of what novels have traditionally narrated as against what they may or should narrate. As she puts it in Chapter 15 – which was the first chapter of the original *Middlemarch* and where she had first invoked Fielding – with regard to one of her heroes, Dr. Lydgate's story:

> We are not afraid of telling over and over again how a man comes to fall in love with a woman and be wedded to her, or else be fatally parted from her. Is it due to excess of poetry or of stupidity that we are never weary of describing what King James called a woman's 'makdom and her fairnesse', never weary of listening to the twanging of the old Troubadour strings, and are comparatively uninterested in that other kind of 'makdom and fairnesse' which must be wooed with industrious thought and patient renunciation of small desires?
>
> (Bk. 2, Ch. 15, 98)

The passion for a larger, an epic destiny, a world-altering passion, which, in Lydgate's case, is a passion for scientific discovery leading to a revolution in medical science.

The epic paradigm for her second protagonist, Dorothea Brooke, is outlined in the 'Prelude' through the example of St. Theresa, the 16th-century Spanish girl (1515–82) who joined the Church, whose heart, as George Eliot puts it, beat from the outset 'to a national idea' demanding 'an epic life', and who, though thwarted at first by 'domestic reality . . . in the shape of uncles', eventually 'found her epos in the reform of a religious order' (xiii).

Now here are these two anti-Fielding paradigms. Why 'comic epic'? Why not 'epic' per se? Why not protagonists whose fable involves not only their destinies but *all* our destinies? In Dorothea's case as much as in Lyd-gate's, however, the paradigm functions in the end only as a sad or tragic underlining of their actual life-struggles. For these latter-day Theresas, although equally imbued with passionate epic inspiration, accomplish no epic destiny, no 'far-resonant action' or 'long-recognizable deed' (xiii–xiv). They become the founders and foundresses of nothing and their stories, too, get reduced to the personal and the domestic.

Invariably a modern reader asks, 'Why?' George Eliot did not write lengthy prefaces in the manner of Fielding. As she says, he lived in an ample age 'when the days were longer . . . when summer afternoons were spacious, and the clock ticked slowly in the winter evenings'. If 'belated historians' like herself lingered 'after his example', their 'chat' would prob-ably sound 'thin and eager'. And in any case she had work enough to show the weaving and interweaving of the many 'human lots' that constitute the web of life that she calls *Middlemarch* (Bk. 2, Ch. 15, 96). Indeed, it is the specific working out of character, circumstance and destiny in *Middle-march*, it is the novel itself rather than the authorial commentary, which constitutes a critical intervention on this issue of the comic-domestic versus the epic, at an appropriate moment in the development of the English novel, exactly midway between Fielding's time and our own age. *Middlemarch* may thus be said to embody in itself as a novel, both a challenge to and an acceptance of a limited domain for the novel.

Discursively, the answer to the question 'Why?' is given in the last two pages – that though potentially epoch-making personalities continue to be born, 'the medium in which their ardent deeds took shape is for ever gone'. Epoch-making is no longer possible; the modern world, it would seem, defeats all aspiration to fundamental world alteration. Historic deeds being impossible, the only hope for the future lies in what George Eliot calls the 'diffusive' influence of examples and individual good deeds, of small unhis-torical changes:

> For the growing good of the world is partly dependent on unhistoric acts; and that things are not so ill with you and me as they might have been, is half owing to the number who lived faithfully a hidden life, and rest in unvisited tombs.

> (Bk. 8, Finale, 577–78)

One would be sorely tempted at this point to start to trace the rise and fortunes of liberal humanism in British political thought and practice in the 19th and 20th centuries, or trace the diminution or, indeed, the privatization, of the novel's domain from E.M. Forster's well-known valorization of per-sonal relations, the famous, 'If I had to choose between betraying my friend or my country, I hope God gives me the guts to betray my country' (*Two Cheers for Democracy*, 66) – an absolute opposition between the individual and the polis – to his less-known declaration earlier in the essay, 'I believe in personal relationships' (66) for 'Here is something solid in a world full of violence and cruelty' (65). Or we could think of D.H. Lawrence's explorations of the sexual experience and the sexual ethic and go on to the interior explorations of the so-called stream-of-consciousness novel.

But it is time to retrace my steps and, more important, call a halt to this one-sided argumentation and go back to the polarities of the novel's domain, the polarities of the individual/collective, private/public, psychological/social, biographical/cultural, domestic/national, topical/historical/universal, etc., and see how its diminutions also become at the same time enhancements of various kinds with regard to the novelists just mentioned.

Joyce's hugely comic novel of consciousness, *Ulysses*, is not only titled after, but alludes constantly to, and reinvents, so to speak, one of the two or three founding epics of Western civilization. As the novelist, the artist as a young man, says on the very last page of *that* preceding novel (*A Portrait of the Artist as a Young Man*): 'Welcome, O life! I go to encounter for the millionth time the reality of experience and to forge in the smithy of my soul the uncreated conscience of my race', juxtaposing 'reality' and 'race' on the one hand with 'soul' and 'conscience' on the other. D.H. Lawrence's novels, notorious for the sex in them, are perhaps still more interesting in my view as novels of cultural and class differentials. As for E.M. Forster, his novels are first and last novels of culture-conflict and mutual critique – Southern Italy and Northern England in *Where Angels Fear to Tread*; India and Britain, the oriental and the Western, in *A Passage to India*; Sawston in *Where Angels Fear to Tread*, as a metonymic representation of the arid, benevolent, narrow-minded British middle-class; or the theme of philistinism versus culture, the Wilcoxes versus the Schlegels, in *Howard's End*, the house, Howard's End, itself standing for Forster's view of the British heritage as the fusion, the connecting, rather than the conflict of classes and cultures. And, finally, *Middlemarch*, wonderful as it is as a collection of at least six individual stories, is still more wonderful for the weaving and interweaving that creates the sense of a whole world that she calls 'A Study of Provincial Life', and which the George Eliot scholar, Gordon Haight, tells us was described to him by a famous historian as 'the finest picture he knew of England at the time of the Reform Bill' (Introduction, vi).

I am now going back to Fielding and the other novels written between his time and George Eliot's and the fascinating means and mechanisms, the formal devices, used by various novelists to manage the polarities, phrased in the seemingly endless pairs of words I mentioned earlier, and resolve them: typologies of various kinds, allegories, symbolisms, metonymies;

'House Novels' like Jane Austen's *Mansfield Park* and *Northanger Abbey*, Emily Brontë's *Wuthering Heights*, Hawthorne's *The House of the Seven Gables*; 'Family Sagas' like Thomas Mann's *Buddenbrooks*, dealing with the German merchant middle-classes, or John Galsworthy's *The Forsythe Saga*, which become class explorations. And, indeed, as readers of novels we should ask ourselves: Whether or not we are conscious of it, in the love stories, the personal stories, the involvement with the hero or heroine, or the empathy with the hero and the heroine, in those works we consider powerful or significant, are we not looking for something beyond the individual and the particular situation to the representation of some larger collective entity, a whole epoch or social order?

Of the means used by novelists to this end, the best known perhaps is the theory of types, originated by the Russian democratic, revolutionary critic, Belinsky, in the mid-19th century, developed by his successor, Dobrolyubov,[2] most memorably in his long essay 'What Is Oblomovitis?' and made famous in the 20th century by Georg Lukacs, the Hungarian Marxist literary historian and critic, in *Studies in European Realism*. Originally developed from and applied to the classic Russian novel of the 19th century, this theory will be more directly useful in my second lecture where a large part of the discussion will focus on Russian fiction. Here, let me just say that Belinsky's theory was not the only way for novelists to resolve polarities. Indeed, my subject being the English novel today, I would at this point like to revert to Henry Fielding and look at this aspect of his novel and a few others.

I have already cited Fielding's definition of the novel as 'a newspaper of many volumes'. I would now like to add to it the following from the American novelist Hawthorne's Preface to *Mosses from an Old Manse*: 'A work of genius is but the newspaper of a century, or perchance of a hundred centuries' (22). A hundred centuries, 10,000 years, pretty much defines not just the domain of literature but the time frame of human civilization itself. But Hawthorne's observation has the merit of suggesting *all* the possibilities of representation available to the novelist *and* all the possible interpretive preferences available to the reader.

To gloss the Hawthorne quotation:

The newspaper, as in Fielding, would signify the daily life of ordinary persons which the novelist would represent, with varying degrees of subtlety, on the individual-moral-psychological plane.

The 'newspaper of a century' would involve the socio-historical plane, epic or epoch-making actions and deeds, as in George Eliot's definition. A 'hundred centuries' signifies, of course, the subject universal, the eternal verities so fondly and freely derided by present-day scholars in the humanities. Nevertheless, it should be pointed out that novelists themselves, like

Hawthorne, stress precisely this universal-eternal plane as the essential plane of their representation. And, to my mind, instead of dismissing summarily one or the other of these planes, the more interesting critical exercise for the student of literature, as I suggested by referring to the theory of types a little earlier, is to see the specific process whereby representations on one plane get translated into another.

For instance, to revert to Fielding, he declares in the very first prefatory chapter of *Tom Jones* that his subject is HUMAN NATURE, all capitalized (Bk. 1, Ch. 1, 25). But what we have to see is how this human nature in general gets transformed into a combination of the moral and the socio-historical, and how, though he himself emphasizes the individual aspect throughout, *Tom Jones* comes across equally as an epic. Not epic in the sense of panoramic, encompassing time and space on a large scale, varying the scene from the country to the road to London finally, and finding accommodation for all sorts and conditions of men to crowd the scenes and incidents of his story, but epic more in the sense of a socio-historical portrait of mid-18th-century society, of which I would like to emphasize two related aspects.

1   The socio-historic is not presented as a bonus, something added over and above the moral-individual, but precisely through his generous yet searching moral analysis of individuals which operates as a diagnostic test of the larger social world in which his individual characters live and function.
2   As a consequence, the portrait, his picture of the epoch, becomes essentially, though not radically, a critical picture.
3   In elucidating this, I shall focus, rather narrowly, on the love and marriage theme in *Tom Jones* and other novels and how through the domestic we get the representation of the epoch.

In *Tom Jones* this theme translates into two different things, simultaneous but different. On the one hand we have his love ethic as apart from his general philanthropic ethics and, on the other, his prudential ethic which itself translates into the acquisitive, the avaricious, the mercenary, and is seen in almost everyone except a few exceptional characters. As the heroine of a later novel, Elizabeth Bennet in Jane Austen's *Pride and Prejudice*, puts it: 'what is the difference in matrimonial affairs, between the mercenary and the prudent motive? Where does discretion end and avarice begin?' (Bk. 2, Ch. 4, 102). This difference between 'discretion' and 'avarice' is precisely the subject of Fielding's ironic motive analysis poised throughout *Tom Jones*. In this context, the Tom-Sophia love story, though in itself one of the finest stories of love in English fiction, becomes also thus a test for the world that surrounds them. It is, as Middleton Murry described it once, 'a thread of gold running through the sordid texture of society' (40).

Fielding has been much praised for his irony. But its pervasive use, and the function that it thus performs in representing, not just individual motivation, but rather the collective portrait of the society of his time, has not been properly understood. For irony is his chief device for the fusing of the one and the many, the individual and the social, the comic common-place and the historically significant. Irony at the simple linguistic level is the expression of one's meaning by language of opposite contradictory tendency, but this verbal irony is the least part of his narratorial strategy. More important is his ironic motive analysis which constantly exposes from beneath people's professions their real and sordid motivations. But the most important aspect of Fielding's irony involves a different kind of doubleness altogether, a different kind of play between opposition and sameness.

It is often said that Fielding's novel is crowded. It is – but it is crowded not just by variety but by opposites, the opposite positions of the characters representing the two sides of some of the central political, social, intellec-tual and religious debates of the 18th century: Whig and Tory; Court and Country; the uncouth, fiercely independent country squire, Squire Western, and his sister, the sophisticated court lady, Mrs. Western, the advocate of women's freedom; Dr. Blifil, the divine, and his brother, Captain Blifil, of the militia; the two tutors, Thwackum, the narrow-minded religious zealot, and Square, the deistic philosopher, believer not in scriptural revelation but 'the rule of right' and 'the eternal fitness of things' (Bk. 3, Ch. 3, 83), and so on. Yet underneath this superficial diversity and mutual opposition, there is an essential sameness or identity of motivation and purpose. They all belong to what may be called the Party of Prudence – that is, avarice and self-seeking – together with most other characters in *Tom Jones*, from the gamekeepers and maidservants and innkeepers to diverse London men and women of wealth and fashion.

Only one illustration will have to suffice, and that, too, bearing on the theme of money and marriage only as relating to the case of Tom and Sophia. Think of the main fable: should Sophia marry Tom or Blifil? Squire Western, her tyrannical father, locks her up. Mrs. Western, his freedom-loving sister, declares that Englishwomen are not like Spanish slaves and should be given their liberty. But however opposing their personalities may be, their views, methods, purpose and motivation, are the same: both are equally determined to prevent Sophia's marrying the fortuneless Tom and, instead, coerce her into marriage with the legal heir of the biggest estate in the neighbourhood.

For, as Squire Western puts it, 'certainly the two estates are . . . joined together in matrimony already' (Bk. 6, Ch. 2, 180) and so, therefore, as we may put it, should the livestock on them. As to Mrs. Western, she begins proceedings by reading Sophia

> a long lecture on the subject of matrimony; which she treated not as a romantic scheme of happiness arising from love, as it hath been described by the poets; nor did she mention any of those purposes for which we are taught by divines to regard it as instituted by sacred authority; she considered it rather as a fund in which prudent women deposit their fortunes to the best advantage, in order to receive a larger interest for them than they could have elsewhere.
>
> (Bk. 7, Ch. 3, 215)

Seven hundred pages later, right at the end of the novel, we find her still lecturing her niece on 'prudence and matrimonial politics' (Bk. 16, Ch. 7, 559), still discoursing 'on the folly of love, and the wisdom of legal prostitution for hire' (Bk. 16, Ch. 8, 563). It is thus by revealing the sameness, the same sordid motivation in a large array of diverse, mutually opposed human beings, by a pervasive, constant analysis, that Fielding's irony weaves, thread by thread, the sordid texture of society itself, so that the moral analysis itself so accumulates, so overcomes, differences of personality, that it becomes itself a diagnostic test of society.

I shall now turn to two novels of the 19th century, *Dombey and Son* and *Vanity Fair*, in order to see where these signposts hung out so early by Fielding in *Tom Jones* lead us in the domain of the novel, keeping in mind all three possible terrains of the individual-moral, the socio-historical, and the universal, the emphasis being on the means by which they try to resolve or fail to resolve these possibilities, to the point that some of these novels become openly recognizable – and are indeed commonly recognized – as 'pictures of society', not so much a moral critique as in Fielding but rather a representation through individual stories of the very structure of 19th-century British bourgeois society.

First of all, the intrusion I noted in *Tom Jones* of the language of money and commerce into the language of love and marriage not only continues into the 19th century but becomes a pervasive conflation with enlarged application and meaning. Here, although I shall talk of Jane Austen's *Emma* in my second lecture, in an effort to enliven proceedings a little, I should like to begin by quoting the following, rather cavalier description of Jane Austen by Auden in his poem 'Letter to Lord Byron, Part I'. Auden speaks wryly of how 'uncomfortable' he feels to see 'An English spinster of the middle-class / Describe the amorous effects of "brass" ', and reveal the 'economic basis of society' (84).

Brass and Amour, Money and Love. Leaving aside the exceptional case that the 19th-century novelists continue to include as exemplum, the mercenary motivation of marriage is now no longer seen as brazen but as the commonplace acceptable norm.

But something of much larger importance than just marriage is involved in *Dombey and Son* and *Vanity Fair* which I shall indicate by, first, quoting the following from *Vanity Fair*: George Osborne's description of *Vanity Fair* as a 'ready-money society' (Ch. 20, 195); Becky Sharp's declaration, 'I think I could be a good woman if I had five thousand a year' (Ch. 41, 409) and 'I wish I could exchange my position in society, and all my relations for a snug sum in the three percent Consols' (Ch. 41, 410). And more significantly, Osborne Senior's outburst: 'Honourables? Damn Honourables. I am a plain British merchant I am: and could buy the beggarly hounds over and over' (Ch. 42, 414). And finally this from the Marquis of Steyne to Becky when she seeks through him to gain an entry into the world of these very 'honourables' – the gentry, the nobility and indeed the Court itself: 'You won't be able to hold your own there, you silly little fool. You've got no money' (Ch. 48, 465). Not no title, no gentility, no blue blood, no pedigree, no genealogy, but no MONEY. The enlargement of significance that I spoke of comes to this, then: money and commerce as the basis of not just marriage but of morality at one end – 'I could be a GOOD woman if I had five thousand a year' – and finally, at the other end, the macro level, as the basis of *all* family and social relations, class interaction and class mobility.

On what makes some of these novels thus the newspapers of a century or an epoch, the representation of the structure of a whole society in its historical evolution, I cannot do better than create as a gloss the following from the great 19th-century sociologist Alexis de Tocqueville's *The Old Regime and the French Revolution*:

> It was not merely parliamentary government, freedom of speech, and the jury system that made England so different from the rest of contemporary Europe. There was something still more distinctive and more far-reaching in its effects. England was the only country in which the caste system had been totally abolished, not merely modified. Nobility and commoners joined forces in business enterprises, entered the same professions, and – what is still more significant – intermarried. The daughter of the greatest lord in the land could marry a 'new' man without the least compunction.

(82–3)[3]

Thus, Dickens and Thackeray effect the translation of the individual into the socio-historical by:

One, continuing the theme of love and marriage but now making the matrimonial alliance reflect the class situation in England as observed by Tocqueville: Rose Dawson, the daughter of an Ironmonger, marrying the Squire of Queen's Crawley, Sir Pitt; or Dombey, the City Man, marrying – buying would be the more appropriate word – the daughter of a Westend, shabby-genteel, 'aristocratic' family. So that we now have this curious class interaction which goes, as Tocqueville says, from class activity to marriage, combines the personal and historical, the gentry thus marrying downwards for money and the merchants upwards for gentility, honour, rank and social precedence.

Second, through what may still be called irony, but now not in the shape of Fielding's constant motive analysis of individuals, but in the shape of the ironic juxtaposition of the personal and the familial with the commercial and the social, such as in the title itself of *Dombey and Son* which juxtaposes Dombey's position as the head of a commercial house and his position as the head of a family, especially as the father of a son – the son longed for and prized as the 'capital of the House's name and dignity', the daughter scorned as a 'base coin that could not be invested' (Ch. 1, 51). (Feminists may wish to note the change of imagery in male-chauvinistic rhetoric here from the pastoral times of *Tom Jones* where Captain Blifil describes woman as 'an animal of domestic use', Bk. 2, Ch. 7, 70.)

The most visibly important shift is, of course, the shift from the rural to the urban, the foregrounding of the dominant bourgeoisie and the emergence of merchants, the merchant princes, as the new protagonists. I always recall the short description of Dombey in the Dickens novel as 'a pecuniary Duke of York' (Ch. 1, 58), an epithet that encapsulates the compromise, the Tocquevillian merger of the former antagonistic ruling classes in England.

But let me turn to the much greater novel, Thackeray's *Vanity Fair*. This panoramic, one-sided epic, covering seventeen years of time and space, encompasses the whole of the British Empire: first London, Queen's Crawley, Brussels, the Napoleonic Wars in Europe, then the West Indies, and then all the way to India, to Ram Ganj near Calcutta. The time dimension and space spread seem so enormous that it appears to be almost a loosener. But it is curious how these act like spokes radiating outwards from the hub, and the hub is the city of London, the financial district of London, because in Thackeray we do not have industrial finance but speculative finance. The hub holds all the spokes together, and the novel is finally dominated by the rise and fall and fortunes of the two merchant families, the Osbornes and the Sedleys, and again, through ironic juxtaposition, not just of their commercial fortunes but of their family fortunes, the marrying or not marrying of their sons and daughters.

No wonder that critics have recognized these novels as portraits of their own epoch. Barbara Hardy sees the 19th-century English novel as sociology and describes Thackeray as a 'great sociologist', 'a great accumulator of social symbols of class and money' (20). While this is no doubt true of Thackeray, it is also totally inadequate, totally dependent on external symbolization and totally unaware of the subtle ways in which he fuses the individual with the social, the inner with the outer, the psychological with the sociological. If I were to call him a sociologist, I would rather align him with the modern sociologists who are theorists of ideology. He ranks in my book among the novelists who may be called pre-Althusser Althusserians. But of this, more in my last lecture.

Curiously enough, this aspect of Thackeray, nowhere to be found in modern criticism of him, is hinted at by two of his oldest and most old-fashioned critics. One was his contemporary, W.C. Roscoe, who in an 1856 essay says:

> The social human heart . . . that is [Thackeray's] subject. His actors are distinct and individual . . . but the personal character of each is not the supreme object of interest with the author. . . . Man is his study; but man the social animal.
>
> (267)

Roscoe's 'social animal' almost becomes the ideological animal in the next critic W.C. Brownell's 1902 essay, almost but not quite, largely because Brownell does not have the word 'ideology' at hand and makes do with the word 'idea' instead:

> Thackeray's personages are never portrayed in isolation. They are a part of the milieu in which they exist. . . . Their activities are modified by the air they breathe in common. Their conduct is controlled, their ideas affected, even their desires and ambitions dictated by the general ideas of the society that includes them.
>
> (29)

For its time, not a bad formulation of the idea that individuals, subjects – their conduct, ideas, desires – are constituted by subjection to ideology, in Brownell's phrase, 'the general ideas of the society that includes them'.

While this is the crux of the matter, how individual stories function as pictures of an epoch, how the diminution becomes an enhancement, I feel something more needs to be said, by and to those who wish to consider *developments* and transformations within literary traditions and take note of not only the dominant but also, however briefly, of the residual and the vanishing. This is incumbent upon me, at least, who began with the idea of not two but three possible planes of representation open to the novelist, not just individual and social but also universal, and promised besides to take into account the novelist's own definition of his chosen realm or realms.

If Fielding comes before us as a moralist whose subject was HUMAN NATURE, Dickens in his letter to Forster outlining plans for *Dombey and Son* declares that it 'was to do with Pride', an eternal failing of man (471), and Thackeray in his constant, and often irritating authorial commentary, makes his novel out to be a meditation on the vanity of human wishes: 'Vanitas vanitatum – all is vanity, saith the preacher', and, indeed, I do sense when I read *Vanity Fair* that *Ecclesiastes* or the Book of the Preacher is one of the sourcebooks or inspirations behind his narratorial stance in *Vanity Fair*.[4] Vanity in this sense, like Fielding's HUMAN NATURE, is a universal category, as is Pride the way Dickens means it in his outline.

I have already commented on the ambiguity of Dickens's title as a conjunction of the commercial and the familial. Thackeray's title combines the commercial with the universal, the Fair which means the marketplace with Vanity. Thackeray's subtitles are, no doubt, clear and state his subject as we understand it: *Pen and Pencil Sketches of English Society* in the serial form, and, in the final version, *A Novel Without a Hero* – which comes to the same thing, inasmuch as it is a collective portrait, a portrait not of individual heroes but of the whole society which he calls *Vanity Fair*.

But what do we say, then, about the ambiguities, the complicating universals? What we may say suggests itself, I think, if we finally note a further ambiguity, the ambiguity of the narrative persona in *Vanity Fair*, which, let me remind you, is that of the Clown even more than that of the Preacher in the *Ecclesiastes*, and to which persona he draws attention by his sketch on the cover of the novel as published in monthly parts, and whom he glosses in pen within the novel as not wearing the gown and bands and the shovel hat of the Preacher but the long-eared livery and the cap and bells of the Clown. And yet as he observes, Preacher or Clown, the function of both in telling bitter truths remains the same.

In this, Thackeray anticipates by a hundred years the Polish philosopher Leszek Kolakowski's well-known essay, 'The Priest and the Clown: Reflections on the Theological Heritage in Modern Thinking'.[5] The function performed earlier by the priest is now performed by the clown so that what we may say finally about the novels I have been considering is something like the following:

What these early English novels do is to start with traditional moral-universal categories – human nature, pride, vanity – and redefine them in terms of contemporary, material realities, so that what we see in them is

(a) a residue of, and an internal struggle with the older modes of thought as well as older modes and subjects of literature, and (b) at the same time, heightened by this internal struggle, to break free from older modes of thought, a more central accomplishment, the representation of the socio-historical in terms that come close to our own understanding and expectations of what great novels do, and in what a theoretically wide-open, heterogeneous, anarchic domain.

Notes

1 This oft-quoted line is from Benjamin Harris's 1690 *The New England Primer*. Harris (1673–1716), an English publisher who published anti-Catholic pamphlets, was a figure in the Popish plot, a conspiracy invented by Titus Oates which resulted in anti-Catholic hysteria in England between 1678 and 1681. He moved to Boston in 1686 where he established a successful bookstore and coffeehouse. He returned to London and journalism in 1695, and his *London Post* appeared regularly from 1699 to 1706.
2 Belinsky and Dobrolyubov, very influential 19th-century Russian literary critics, are discussed in the second lecture, 'Nationality and the Novel', where a detailed note on them appears.
3 Alexis Charles-Henri-Maurice Clerel, Viscount de Tocqueville (1805–59), born of a noble family, active in French politics serving briefly as Minister of Foreign Affairs after the Revolution of 1848, is best known as a political scientist and historian for his works *Democracy in America* (2 volumes) and *The Old Regime and the French Revolution* (1856) which analyzes French society before the Revolution, investigates the forces that led to it, and stresses its importance in continuing the process of modernizing France. Tocqueville studied English history as a model of political development.
4 Thackeray's title is taken from John Bunyan's allegory *The Pilgrim's Progress* (1678), where Christian, in the course of his journey from the City of Destruction to the Celestial City, comes to a town called Vanity Fair built by Beelzebub, where all year round houses, honours, preferments, titles and pleasures are traded.
5 Leszek Kolakowski (1927–2009), Polish philosopher and historian of ideas, was expelled from his professorship in Warsaw for political reasons and subsequently taught at Oxford, rejected Marxism, helped inspire the Solidarity movement in Poland and turned in his later writings to religion. His essay was made known by Jan Kott, who translated a key part and applied it to his reading of *King Lear*.

Works cited

Auden, W.H. 'Letter to Lord Byron' (1936). *The Collected Poems*. Ed. Edward Mendelson. London: Faber and Faber, 1976, rpt. 2007.
Austen, Jane. *Mansfield Park*. London: Penguin Books, 1988.
———. *Pride and Prejudice*. Ed. Donald Gray. London and New York: W.W. Norton & Co., 2001.
———. *Northanger Abbey*. New York: Pearson and Longman, 2005.

Brontë, Emily. *Wuthering Heights*. London: Penguin Books, 1988.

Brownell, W.C. *Victorian Prose Masters*. New York: Charles Scribner's Sons, 1902.

Defoe, Daniel. *Moll Flanders*. Ed. Paul A. Scanlon. Peterborough, ON: Broadview Press, 2005.

Dickens, Charles. *Dombey and Son*. Ed. Peter Fairclough, Introduction Raymond Williams. Harmondsworth, Middlesex: Penguin Books, 1970.

Eliot, George. *Middlemarch*. Ed. Bert G. Hornbach. New York: W.W. Norton & Co., 1977.

Fielding, Henry. *Joseph Andrews and Shamela*. Ed. Sheridan Baker. New York: Thomas Y. Crowell Company, 1972.

———. *Tom Jones*. Ed. Sheridan Baker. New York: W.W. Norton & Co., 1973, rpt. 1995.

Forster, E.M. *Howard's End*. London: Edward Arnold, 1947.

———. *Where Angels Fear to Tread*. London: Edward Arnold, 1947.

———. 'What I Believe'. *Two Cheers for Democracy*. London: Edward Arnold, 1951.

———. *A Passage to India*. London: Edward Arnold, 1978.

Forster, John. *The Life of Charles Dickens*. New York: Doubleday, 1928.

Galsworthy, John. *The Forsythe Saga*. London: Heinemann, 1922.

Haight, Gordon S. Ed. *Middlemarch*. Boston: Houghton Mifflin Company, 1956, rpt. 1968.

Hardy, Barbara. *The Exposure of Luxury: Radical Themes in Thackeray*. London: Peter Owen, 1972.

Hawthorne, Nathaniel. *Mosses from an Old Manse*. New York: Hovendon, n.d.

———. *The House of the Seven Gables*. See Works Cited, Ch. 4.

Joyce, James. *A Portrait of the Artist as a Young Man*. London: Jonathan Cape, 1916.

———. *Ulysses*. Ed. Rainer Emig. Houndmills and Basingstoke, Hampshire: Macmillan, 2004.

Kolakowski, Leszek. 'The Priest and the Clown: Reflections on the Theological Heritage in Modern Thinking'. *Tworczosc No. 10* (1959), 82–3 (in Polish). Quoted by Jan Kott, *Shakespeare Our Contemporary*. Tr. Boleslaw Taborski. Preface by Peter Brook. London: Methuen, 1965.

Lukacs, Georg (Gyorgy). *Studies in European Realism*. With an Introduction by Alfred Kazin. New York: The Universal Library, Grossart & Dunlap, 1964.

Mann, Thomas. *Buddenbrooks*. Cambridge: Cambridge University Press, 1987.

Middleton-Murry, John. 'In Defence of Fielding'. *Unprofessional Essays*. London: Jonathan Cape, 1956.

Richardson, Samuel. *Pamela*. Introduction by Kinkead-Weekes. London: Dent, 1962.

Roscoe, W.C. 'W.M. Thackeray, Artist and Moralist'. *National Review*, January 1856. rpt. *William Thackeray: The Critical Heritage Series*. Ed. Geoffrey Tillotson and Donald Hawes. London: Routledge & Kegan Paul, 1968, pp. 265–85.

Shakespeare, William. *King Lear*. Ed. Kenneth Muir. London: Methuen, 1952, rpt. 1961, 1966.

Shelley, Percy Bysshe. 'Adonais'. *Shelley's Poetry and Prose*. Ed. Donald Reiman and Sharon B. Powers. New York and London: W.W. Norton & Co., 1977.

Thackeray, W.M. *Vanity Fair*. Ed. with an Introduction and Notes. Geoffrey and Kathleen Tillotson. Boston: Houghton Mifflin Company, 1963.

Tocqueville, Alexis de. *The Old Regime and the French Revolution*. Tr. Stuart Gilbert. New York: Doubleday, 1955.

2   Nationality and the novel

Today I shall be bringing together a clutch of novels from different countries under the rubric of 'national epics' – novels which still tell the personal and domestic stories of ordinary individuals, not historical personages, but whose other pole is now defined, more or less consciously, as nationality.

This involves, first of all, a definition of the term 'nationality' and a summary of the historical emergence in Western Europe of what are called nations or nation-states everywhere in the world today.

But there is here at the outset a polarity within a polarity, a conflation or confluence in the term nationality itself or two distinct concepts. One is the ancient and somewhat nebulous concept of 'natio' with the same root meaning as 'native' and 'nativity' signifying where one is born, a micro-entity, family, domicile, local community, the condition of belonging. As Raymond Williams puts it:

> 'Nation', as a term, is radically connected with 'native'. We are *born* into relationships, which are typically settled in a place. This form of primary and 'placeable' bonding is of quite fundamental human and natural importance. Yet the jump from that to anything like the modern nation-state is entirely artificial.
>
> (180)

The second, what has happened in modern times is, in Williams's words again, 'that the real and powerful feelings of a native place and a native formation have been pressed and incorporated into an essentially political and administrative organization, which has grown from quite different roots' (181).

Before I go on to these different roots, I would like to emphasize this distinction since it will figure in my argument at several points today, the distinction between what I would like to call the hard facts on the one hand – matters of economic, political and administrative organization, a model which 'once created', as Benedict Anderson points out, can be 'transplanted . . . to a great variety of social terrains' (4), a homogenizing force leading ultimately to what Paul Ricoeur has called 'universal civilization' (276–7) – and, on the other, the native, the local, the natural, the kinship bonding, the family and the community.

This distinction has that much more relevance for literature generally, inasmuch as if it reaches out to the general and the universal, it is always in and through the local and the particular, Shakespeare's 'local habitation' and 'name' (*A Midsummer Night's Dream*, V.1.17). With regard to my own subject today, for example, as Belinsky put it in his eighth article on Pushkin, it is only 'in civil and family relations . . . and the exclusive situations of life . . . [that] nationality tells, and a man stands out for what he is – a son of his own and stepson of an alien land' (219).

Returning to the roots of the modern nation-states in Western Europe, these, unlike the ancient 'natio', are relatively easy to identify and locate in history. For the thousand years we call the Middle Ages, Europe was not divided into *nations*. There were different lands, not nations, which were all part of a single system, the Holy Roman Empire or Christendom. There was one common language, Latin, and a common literature in this. National languages were not worth learning or teaching. Vernaculars were the language of slaves and serfs, the root 'verna' meaning a house slave. There was more in common between the knights and clerics of different lands than between the knight and peasant of the same land. There was one common legal code and in the Catholic Church one common religious organization. There were no 'international' wars like the one between England and France in Napoleonic times but only wars between the whole of Christendom and the heathens or infidels.

The break-up of this unity and the formation of modern states took place during the 16th to 18th centuries: territorially, by wars and conquests or by marriages and other alliances; politically, by the emergence of a strong central power; economically, by mercantile activities and the circulation of money; socially, by the rise of the merchant class including primarily merchants and later industrial manufacturers; linguistically, by the emergence of a standardized *national* language from amongst the many local dialects, for example, standard English from the East Midland dialect, together with, simultaneously, the establishment of printing or print capitalism.

These are what I have called hard facts, hard modern realities, and it is their incorporation of the older 'natio', natural in the sense of being humanly inevitable, that makes Williams describe modern nations as 'artificial', Anderson as 'imagined communities', and yet another writer, Timothy Brennan, as 'fictional nations' (1). Many others could be cited, but let me sum up the point by quoting Ernest Gellner, the Cambridge sociologist: 'Nationalism is not the awakening of nations to self-consciousness: it *invents* nations where they do not exist' (169, emphasis added).

As an aside, I find these formulations simplistic and evasive. In what sense, for instance, can we call the hard facts I have enumerated as non-existent? And if nationalism is an invention, so are all historical realities and social formations. The point rather would be to see how the new incorporates the old or the imagined to create a powerful sense of cohesion and national self-consciousness. It is a complex and drawn-out process. It includes the linkage of past tradition with present realities, for instance, projecting modern history as a continuation of legendary history or even mythology and incorporating mythical motifs in national flags and anthems.

But it is time to come to my main purpose in this lecture, which is to see the place of the novel in this process of national self-consciousness or self-imaging, the rise of the novel more or less coinciding historically with the emergence of nationalities.

With regard to the early English novel, mainly of the 18th century, this process has been outlined by other scholars in general and quite interesting terms, the process whereby, in Brennan's phraseology, 'national fictions' both derive from and feed back into the formation of 'fictional nations', that is, the 'culture-work' they do in the internal consolidation and self-definition of nationality. I have already given a whole lecture on the English novel and, besides, I am personally more interested in the question of 'Nationality and the Novel' with regard not to the nations of Western Europe but the case of what I call 'belated nationalities' such as America, Russia, India, where nationalism becomes not only the central but also in itself a contentious issue.

But before turning to these other countries, let me go back to some of what I said last time and gloss it in today's context as follows: it has been said that the English novel while focussing on the middle class does its work in the interests of national unification by, say, introducing characters from other strata to create the sense of a well-centred society, and, indeed, this is true nowhere so preeminently as in *Tom Jones*. Likewise, unification through the line of the narrative which has been described as the movement of the hero through a sociological landscape, horizontally as well as vertically, to create the picture of a cohesive natural society. For the horizontal movement we can think of Fielding's hero, and for the vertical who so prominent a model as Thackeray's Becky Sharp. But at this point I would like to focus on just one English novel. Combining the idea of vertical movement with another feature of 'national fictions', their portrayals of somehow distinctively national codes of family nurture and daily conduct, Belinsky's 'civil and family relations' in which alone nationality tells, I would like to rehearse briefly one aspect of Jane Austen's *Emma* as highlighted by Lionel Trilling.

Emma is a novel about love, marriage and social intercourse generally between a few village families in a small nondescript corner of England. It is a paradigm of what is called the 'Comedy of Manners'. At this level the heroine, an otherwise attractive and enviable girl, is shown to be blemished by vanity – not personal vanity, but rather a combination of snobbery and a hyperactive imagination, blemishes that lead her into a series of blunders until, presumably chastened and subdued, she is rewarded with the custom-ary happy marriage at the end. Yet, as Trilling says, this quiet domestic novel seems to be 'touched . . . by national feeling' (xii), by a tendency to conceive of a specifically *English* ethic as, for instance, in the description of Frank Churchill as 'amiable' only in French, not in English – 'he can have no English delicacy towards the feelings of other people' (Bk. 1, Ch. 18, 115).

But the Englishness of *Emma* goes deeper than the surface of manners and, through the theme of marriage itself, reflects upon what Tocqueville, you will recall, saw as the distinctive social structure in England at the time of the French Revolution, the social mobility of a system in which, unlike in France, 'Nobility and commoners joined forces in business enterprises and – what is still more significant – intermarried'. In the next paragraph Tocqueville goes on to say:

> Though this curious revolution (for such in fact it was) is hidden in the mists of time, we can detect traces of it in the English language. For several centuries the word 'gentleman' has had in England a quite different application from what it had when it originated . . . we find its connotation being steadily widened in England as the classes draw nearer to each other and intermingle. In each successive century we find it being applied to men a little lower in the social scale.
>
> (83)

Seen in this context, Emma's snobbery becomes class snobbery.

As you will recall, the social order underlying the matrimonial plot of Emma comprises the gentry represented by the three country seats – Mr. Knightley's Donwell Abbey, Mr. Woodhouse's Hartfield, and Mr. Weston's Randalls; much below them the merchant class represented by the Coles and, still farther below, the independent English farmer, Robert Martin, whom Emma calls a yeoman. While she accepts not only Mr. Knightley but Mr. Weston as well on equal footing, she is condescending towards the Coles (the merchant family), forgetting that Mr. Weston came of a family which only during the 'last two or three generations had been rising into gentility and property' (Bk. 1, Ch. 2, 8) and had himself engaged in trade to make the money which finally enabled him to buy his country seat.

But her worst mistake, a mistake that takes the plot of the novel close to the tragic, is her attitude to Robert Martin who is already a 'gentleman-farmer', as Knightley calls him (Bk. 1, Ch. 8, 46), and rising higher in prosperity by the year, but whom Emma considers beneath her notice on principle or, as she says, 'The yeomanry are precisely the order of people with whom I feel I can have nothing to do' (Bk. 1, Ch. 4, 20). Well might Trilling call this 'a mistake of nothing less than national import' (xii), for she is denying the very process that Tocqueville thought made English society so different from the French. But Jane Austen knows better. *Her* description of Englishness – 'English verdure, English culture [agriculture], English comfort' (Bk. 3, Ch. 1, 282) – puts the gentleman farmer close to the centre.

Let me now turn to what I have called 'belated nationalities', belated entrants into the historical process I have outlined, comprising (a) the formation of the nation in the 'hard' sense and (b) more to my purpose, the cultivation of a sense of distinctive nationality, and, with that, (c) the need for a distinctive national literature. If we keep all three components of the process in mind, of my three examples, Russia and America (that is, the United States) may be said to enter into this whole process in the 1830s and India later in the 19th and early 20th century. I may add at the outset, by way of preface, that my emphasis will be all on difference: (a) the difference between these three on the one hand and, on the other, the Western European model; (b) the differences among these three – Russia, America, India – themselves; and (c) ultimately for my subject, the difference these differentials make with regard to the early novel in these three countries in the matter of their central concerns and conflicts, their form and their creation of national archetypal characters, and often even typical locales or localities which, by synecdoche, come to represent some significant aspect if not the whole of the national condition. I may further add that given the material and the time in hand, my discussion of the novel in each of the three cases will focus on these general aspects rather than any detailed analysis of individual novels.

There was not much difference in terms of the 'hard' realities of economic and political transformation or modernization between these countries and the Western model. The United States was, in fact, an effortless extension of that model with the added advantage that, unlike Europe, it had no feudal past with which to contend. Russia was, by contrast, all feudal, but then modernization had begun there in the early 18th century, symbolized by Peter the Great and the city he built on the marshland of the river Neva as a 'window on the West', its name therefore now appropriately reverted from Leningrad to St. Petersburg again. In short, Western nationalism, translatable to other social terrains as Benedict Anderson observed, was so translated at different periods in the 19th century.

But while this is true of the hard model, what about Anderson's own concept of nations as imagined communities? For, as Partha Chatterjee puts it in *The Nation and Its Fragments: Colonial and Post-Colonial Histories*: 'If nationalisms in the rest of the world have to choose their imagined community from certain "modular" forms already made available to them by Europe and the Americas, what do they have left to imagine?' Chatterjee is thinking clearly of the *modern* West as a bloc (Europe and the Americas) as against the Afro-Asian bloc but, nevertheless, what he goes on to say about the latter applies also to countries within the Western bloc: 'the nationalist imagination in Asia and Africa [is] posited not on an identity but rather on a *difference* with the "modular" forms of national society propagated by the modern West' (5).

It is, indeed, at this level, the level of the nationalist *imagination* rather than the level of hard facts that I find the story of belated nationalities more complex, and their discourse, both political and literary, richer, more radical in some ways, more contentious and problematic, than the internally self-defining, homogenizing discourse of Western European nationalism. I shall come to the specifics of my three chosen examples in a moment, but let me say here that they share much in common if only because in their case nationality could not be simply an internal self-definition. The Western model was already there as a compelling, inescapable, *external* point of reference or conflicting presence. So was the natio and the native, not easily harmonizable with the imported model of nationality but often resistant, like a polar opposite, leading to a debate or a dialectic rather than an easy cohesion between the two, the native both resisting and yet accepting the Western nationalist imagination.

In the literary field we thus have, on the one hand, Emerson's call in the 1830s for the creation of a national, totally American literature, his famous 'We have listened too long to the courtly muses of Europe' (36), paralleled by a similar appeal later *To the Young Generation* (1861) by Shelgunov and Mikhailov: 'We have aped the French and the Germans quite enough. Do we need to ape the English as well?' (quoted in Joseph Frank, 333).[1] On the other hand, we have Henry James in a letter to Charles Eliot Norton dated February 4, 1872: 'It's a complex fate, being an American, and one of the responsibilities it entails is fighting against a superstitious valuation of Europe' (93); and even Dostoevsky, though a Slavophile, who warned the country against what he called the 'putrefaction of the West', declaring: 'We Russians have two motherlands – Russia and Europe – even in cases where we call ourselves Slavophiles' (*The Diary of a Writer*, 342).

Having cited Dostoevsky, I will turn specifically to the first of my three belated nationalities, though I must make it clear that I shall not mention Dostoevsky again nor that 'Russianness' of his novels which, contra the Western novel, raises apparently grand metaphysical questions about God, the human condition and Holy Russia. As before, I shall concern myself with earlier Russian novels and the national experience.

Russia's exposure to the West, initiated by Peter the Great, became a direct and mass-scale encounter during the Napoleonic invasion and its aftermath when, following the defeat at Moscow in 1812, the Russian army followed the retreating French all the way to Paris. The West became now a reality that affected profoundly both Russian literature and Russian politics. The intelligentsia was split between the two poles of outward-looking, modernizing Westernizers, on the one hand, and, on the other, the inward-backward-looking Slavophiles, valorizers of the Muzhik and the Mir (the peasant and the peasant community), together with the so-called 'official patriots', supporters of the authoritarian establishment grouped under Czar Nicholas the First's triadic doctrine of Aristocracy, Orthodoxy *and* Nationality.[2]

The basic reality was, of course, the stirrings within the Russian feudal order, its centuries-old stagnant serf-culture, of the forces of modernization – industry, commerce, democratic government as represented by the West – and the political responses to it which, beginning with the Decembrist uprising of 1825,[3] varied as the century progressed from reformist prescriptions to various kinds of formulas for revolutionary change.

Thus, while Russia had as long a past, historical and legendary, as Western European nations, it did not merge harmoniously with the new Western model of nationhood. The nationalist imagined the two, rather, as opposites, seeing the new and the Western, quite often, not as a continuation of, but as a menace to, a disruption of, the old, the native, the traditional. And the Russian novel, so far from doing the culture work of promoting a unified national image and creating a cohesive sense of self-consciousness, problematized the idea of nationality along these very lines. Indeed, Russian nationality, its definition and destiny in these terms, became the central concern of Russian novels from Pushkin[4] in the early 1830s to Saltykov-Shchedrin[5] in the late 1870s whose novel *The Golovlyov Family* (published in 1880) shows the declining gentry-landlord-serf-owning class finally and tragically collapsing under the accumulated burden of its long, parasitic, guilt-ridden, existence.

The condition of this class is what Dobrolyubov in his famous essay described as a morbid condition, the result of a long-drawn-out disease which, following Goncharov's novel *Oblomov*, he named *Oblomovitis* and in terms of which he discussed not only Goncharov's hero but a whole line of heroes, from Pushkin's Onegin in whom, as Dobrolyubov observed, we already find 'the generic features of the Oblomov type' (140), to such characters as Lermontov's Pechorin, Herzen's Beltov and Turgenev's Rudin,[6] all representing what Dobrolyubov called 'our native, national type' (140), the type of the idle, indolent, serf-owning class without purpose in life and, therefore, without any outlet for intelligence and energy.

While this is the 'native' national type, Goncharov's novel is also, in Dobrolyubov's phrase, 'a sign of the times' (140), of the historical juncture where the old and the native was confronted by the new and the Western. Behind Dobrolyubov's essay stands the authority of Belinsky,[7] the leader of the school of Russian democratic critics, who once declared it as his 'fundamental conviction that the creation of artistic types indicates through both its positive and negative aspects the road society has taken and the road it should take in the future" (Annenkov, 218).[8]

It is this dialectic within the idea of nationality that the Russian novelists embody, with, it should be added, varying degrees of *divided* rather than one-sided sympathies. The clearest example of this past/future, Russian/ Western, dialectic is, of course, *Oblomov*, but before turning to it I would like to look briefly, in these very terms, at *Eugene Onegin*, Pushkin's verse novel, that Belinsky hailed as Russia's 'first really national poem . . . [which] . . . contains more nationality than any other Russian work' (215–16). He continues, 'Pushkin wrote about Russia for Russia. . . . And that is why his *Onegin* is a supremely original and national Russian creation' (222) and reiterates: '*Onegin* could be called an encyclopaedia of Russian life, and a supremely national work' (294). Russian critics saw in Pushkin's work, to quote John Bayley, 'a masterpiece of social diagnosis. It seemed to them to sum up the situation and the sickness of the age in Russia, and to present its definitive psychological types, alike in their weakness and their strength' (16).

Eugene Onegin, like so many novels, is a story of love and marriage, only in this case not a happy story but rather ironic and even tragic. As in other great novels, the individual's story is also at the same time historically representative as Pushkin sets up in and through it the polarities of the past and the present, Russian and Western. He does this, for example, in the matter of settings, a division between the city and the country and further, between the 'artificial' modern city of Petersburg, on the one hand, and on the other Moscow, associated with the old Muscovy. But he does this mainly by bringing together in an ironic love story the hero and the heroine. On the one side we have Tatyana, who became the prototype for subsequent Russian novelists with her commonplace folk name, whom Belinsky describes as typifying Russian womanhood (292), Dostoevsky as the 'apotheosis' of the Russian woman (quoted in Joseph Frank, 828) and Pushkin himself as that 'profoundly Russian being' (Ch. 5, IV), a country girl representing the customs, manners, family values, folklore and folkways of old Russia. And on the other side, Pushkin's hero Onegin, the prime example of the 'superfluous man', who can find no outlet for his energies in a repressive and autocratic society, the rootless Petersburg dandy, modern and fashionable, egotistical, cynical, associated with the cold northern river Onega as well as with Napoleon, Byron and the West generally, 'mastered', as Pushkin puts it, by 'Russia's *chondria*', so that 'to life [he] grew colder than the dead', 'nothing caused his heart to stir, / and nothing pierced his senses' blur' (Ch. 1, XXXVIII).

From this it might seem that Pushkin's sympathies are all on one side: 'I love my Tatyana too much!'(Ch. 4, XXIV). But actually the overall attitude is far more subtle and the critique, via Onegin, of the stagnant squirearchy, as strong as that of the modern realities, an attitude that results in what may be called a negative critique of negative values leading, not to a positive resolution, but to a question mark: what is the future of Russia as a nation? What does the Western intrusion portend? In novelistic terms: Who or what is Onegin? A 'freakish stranger', from 'heaven' or from 'hell', an 'angel' or a 'devil', an 'apparition', a 'shadow', a 'Muscovite in Harold's [Byron's Childe Harold's] dress'? (Ch. 7, XXIV)?

Similar questions are raised about the disruptive, enigmatic heroes of succeeding novels: who is Pechorin, the Byronic hero of Lermontov's *A Hero of Our Time*? Who is Chichikov in Gogol's *Dead Souls*? A scoundrel, a missile of acquisitive energy and enterprise who, in pursuit of a blatant scam – buying dead serfs on paper for use as collateral for bank loans – lands into and disrupts the placid, corrupt, gourmandizing lives of the landowners and bureaucrats in a nameless provincial town epitomizing the whole of feudal Russia.[9]

This dialectic of the Russian and the Western is most clearly represented in Goncharov's *Oblomov* (1859) which Pisarev, the anarchist revolutionary, described as 'the highest generalization of the pre-reforms squirearchic Russia reached until now in our literature'.[10] In the character of its hero, Oblomov (from Oblomok – a ruined fragment), it presents, indeed, the most richly and memorably developed picture of the type and the typical disease identified by Dobrolyubov. It is sometimes said that the 'type' reading of characters ignores all aspects of a novel except the simplistically socio-historical. This is not true. Dobrolyubov's essay reads the character of Oblomov psychologically as well as sociologically, diagnosing Oblomovitis as infantilism as well as decadence, arrested psychological growth as well as arrested social development. Types, furthermore, are not abstractions. They are images that arise from 'the fullness of the phenomena of life' (139) and become elevated to typicality through the investment in them of 'generic and permanent significance' (137).

Much the same was said by Goncharov himself in a passage in *Better Late Than Never* where he defined the one subject running through his three novels as 'the transition from one epoch of Russian life . . . to another' and his reflection of their phenomena in the typicality of his 'portraits, scenes, minor figures, etc.'. For, as he goes on, 'if the images are typical, they necessarily reflect . . . the epoch in which they live. . . . That is to say, reflected in them . . . are phenomena of social life, and the morals, and the day-to-day life'. He adds, 'And if the artist is himself profound, then they will also exhibit a psychological aspect' (quoted in Freeborn, 137–8).

But why just the psychological and the socio-historical? Why not the universal, too? And, indeed, *Oblomov* can be read, and has been read, as a vision of the human desire or temptation to freedom from all effort, struggle, strenuous labour, a desire for eternal peace and rest comparable to that evoked in Tennyson's 'Lotos Eaters' and the 'Land of Cockaigne'.[11] As Oblomov, who takes ninety pages, the whole of the first book of the novel, to get out of bed, and who for the rest is robed mainly in a dressing gown, says at the end of the novel, he, indeed, knew at last why he had been created: 'to show the ideally reposeful aspect of human existence' (Part 4, Ch. 9, 466). But while we may thus interpret Oblomov's indolence and apathy – he is too lazy even to love, which he finds too much like work: 'intimacy with a woman involves a great deal of trouble' (Part 1, Ch. 5, 65) – while we may see him as the type of ideal restfulness, we must remember that this restfulness itself rests on the labour of his house-serf Zakhar and the 300 more Zakhars on his estate, Oblomovka.

Let me sum up these remarks by making two concluding points:

One, not only is Oblomov the richest embodiment of the native type, Goncharov also embodies the other pole of the dialectic through Stoltz, his half-German, Russified friend, who stands for modern enterprise, progress, industry, finance – in short, Western Europe, where he travels extensively in pursuit of his many business enterprises.

Two, unlike earlier novelists, Goncharov suggests a normative resolution to the national question inasmuch as he envisages a future where there are a million Stoltzes but with Russian ('Swadeshi'!) names, leading to the emergence of a composite nationality. The estate of Oblomovka, a synecdoche for Russia, will be modernized but still remain Oblomovka, an estate with serfs, a vague sort of future model held out at the end without any hint of how the basic contradiction is to be resolved.

Let me turn now briefly to the American novel, briefly in view of the fact that the next lecture will be exclusively concerned with American texts. Let me begin by noting the fact that, unlike Russia and India, white American civilization had no past; native Indians and bison did not count, of course. (As Andre Gide once remarked, the true symbol of American civilization is the nickel, the five-cent coin, which bears a bison on the one side and an Indian on the other, both of whom the Americans have successfully exterminated. Which is matched by H.L. Mencken's quip that the pioneering settlers on the American continent fell first on their knees and then on the aborigines!) National consciousness in America, therefore, could not define itself with reference to a native past as one pole and the West as the other. Instead, the emphasis was all on newness *and* the future involving much rhetoric about the repudiation of Europe or the Old World on the one hand and, on the other, defining America or the New World as 'the open frontier of boundless possibility'.

In point of fact, as I said before, America was an extension of Europe, the frontier only a gateway to boundless uninhabited space, a whole available 'new' continent in which to import and establish the European model, its hard realities unimpeded by any old socio-historical structures such as existed in Russia or India. So the newness of the New World was geographical rather than historical, political or social.

But for the early American literary imagination, the matter was not so simple – for literature, no matter is ever simple. ' Romantic', 'Quixotic', 'Visionary', call it what you like, it did take the idea of America as a frontier of boundless possibility seriously enough to create national archetypal scenarios, especially national archetypal characters as distinct from, and even in fundamental opposition to, the typical characters and scenarios of European literature. Such types as Huck Finn, or the tragic Captain Ahab of Melville, or Walt Whitman the hero of *Song of Myself*, a poem that, while insisting on the self, becomes a definition of national identity, a new democracy that ultimately includes the whole world, all nationalities and races and all sorts and conditions of men/women in a new composite brotherhood and sisterhood: 'all the men ever born are also my brothers, and the women my sisters and lovers, / And . . . a kelson of the creation is love' (*Song of Myself*, Section 5).

There are no middle-class epics or heroes here but rather marginal characters, frontier characters they may be called because of their negative, critical relation to establishment values such as marriage, family, property *and*, in the American context, *racism*. If, thus, one had to single out one national archetypal character that stands at the pole from the types of European nationality it would be this *figure poised on the frontier*, not a hero traversing sociological space and unifying it, but one that, leaving the whole of established society behind, moves constantly farther and farther away from it into the open westward wilderness. This figure and scenario, first created by Fenimore Cooper in his great Leatherstocking Saga, appear in many avatars literal and metaphorical in much later fiction and to this day especially on film in the Westerns.

The paradigm, however, was set by Hector St. John Crevecoeur in *Letters from an American Farmer* (1782).[12] A well-educated Frenchman who served in Canada in Montcalm's army as a cartographer, Crevecoeur later migrated southward to settle on a farm in upstate New York. The book is in the form of twelve letters to a highly placed Englishman who is curious about men and matters in the American colonies. The letters raise questions about American identity and the conditions that determine it: a new social system, new laws and a new economic situation marked by the free availability of land, so that the landless peasants of Europe became freeholders. These letters celebrate the New Man, the new American historical and material situation, and the creation of 'the most perfect society now existing in the world' (Letter III, 29). Scattered through the letters, however, is a sense of reversal, of betrayal, which comes to a head in Letter IX with a visit to Charleston, the meeting with slave-holding planters and the spectacle of a black slave with his eyes gouged out left to die in a cage in the wilderness. Slavery is a denial of all the perfect society stands for, of liberty and economic independence, and an assertion of rapacity, pillage, greed, destructiveness, and James the farmer resolves upon a flight from civilization and into a Red Indian tribe. The new paradigm is the frontiersman, man on the edge of civilization poised for a further flight into a deeper wilderness.

Cooper in *The Pioneers* (1823) fictionalizes the same historical situation and process Crevecoeur outlines. Templeton is a recollection of Cooperstown, founded by the novelist's father in New York State, but represents, by way of synecdoche, the whole of America as Cooper would like to see it grow – a prosperous, expanding, agrarian republic. Cooper's hero, Natty Bumppo, originally a bonded servant but now a free American hunter, is a literal frontiersman belonging to that class of rough pioneers – hunters, trappers, woodchoppers – who, historically, opened up the wilderness for the settlements to follow, the irony of their fate being that they thus made the way for their own extinction, for the end of their pursuits and way of life. This is the basic situation in the Leatherstocking Tales – Natty Bumppo, in company with his lifelong friend, the Indian chieftain Chingachgook, both paving the way and at the same time resisting the westward march of American civilization.

In the first of the five Leatherstocking novels, *The Pioneers* (1823), there is in fact a question as to whom the title refers to – Natty Bumppo the hunter or Judge Temple, the colonizing founder of Templeton, a replica of English squirearchy complete with the Manor House, the Anglican Church, tenant houses, in the process of construction and consolidation at the edge of the American wilderness, a transplanted squirearchy on the other side of the Atlantic, a republican squirearchy. At its best there is an evocation of a world in which landlords and tenants, surveyors and labourers, hunters and forest messengers, Indians, Negroes and white settlers, all meet on an equal footing and work together. But beneath the surface a curiously insidious, even sinister note is sounded. Cooper constantly emphasizes that the march of white European civilization involves not only the displacement or marginalization of the class of Natty Bumppos but a deeper, more fundamental and totally irreconcilable conflict: the theme of dispossession, the dispossession of the native Indians, 'the original owners of the land', as he always designated them. It goes beyond legality and involves history itself. The issues are radical: to whom does the land belong? To whom does America belong? Should land belong to men or the other way around?

Such was the force of the historical, social and moral issues raised that Natty becomes the central figure, the hero, of the Leatherstocking saga.[13] While the rest of the cast of characters and the plots are different in each tale, all five of them are held together by Natty and Chingachgook and their lifelong friendship and solidarity. The nature of the Natty-Judge Temple conflict is the same as in Crevecoeur: the conflict between the frontiersman who prepares the way and the farmer who succeeds and eliminates him. But in Cooper the ironic role of the frontiersman is invested with such moral and social questioning that he becomes a resonant, indomitable and also a necessarily tragic figure in a historical drama, suggesting both the inevitability of the developments that actually took place and, at the same time, the lost possibilities of those other forces or ideas which were there, which resisted, but were ultimately overcome by the inexorable logic of history.

At the end, Judge Templeton wins out and Natty sets out westward again, a gesture repeated by his many descendants in American fiction, notably Huck Finn, the most famous and incorrigible repudiator or 'lighter-out'. It is a gesture of repudiation and carries an enormous weight of negative criticism, what Cooper himself felt towards the end of his life when he lost all hope in the distinctive destiny of the new civilization and said in *New York*: 'What is true in the Old World will, in the end, be found to be true here' (61).

But what else does the archetypal Natty's irreconcilable opposition to Western civilization on the one hand and, on the other, his association with Chingachgook and his preference for tribal domicile, tribal ways, tribal social relations, mean? Does it mean a preference, arising out of what Charles Brady calls Cooper's revulsion against 'the dialectics of property' (61), for a sort of primitive, propertyless communism? And, indeed, primitivism, latent or overt, in one form or another, was and remains a tendency or temptation in the American nationalist imagination. But, then, is this a regression from rather than an advance on the Western model, America not as a march into the future but a retreat into the primeval past? Or, is that, indeed, how the imagination conceives it? In a confused, or at least confusing way, does the vision not make the long-lost past an element, somehow, of the future that is to come? This is a problematic issue summed up by Whitman when he asks:

> The friendly and flowing savage, who is he?
>   Is he waiting for civilization, or past it and mastering it?
>
> (*Song of Myself*, Section 39)

Cooper suggests some sort of answer. It must be said that his fascination with tribal life was not confined to its picturesqueness, or to the personal-moral attributes of individual members. It was a counter-vision, and it was positive. It included a preoccupation with tribal social organization and community values, with a life that was not altogether an assault on nature and the native alike, to the point of the depletion of the one and the extermination of the other. It was a life that wounds as well as heals, a life of mutual accommodation. The other positive facet was the relationship between Natty and Chingachgook, the first of three such relationships across racial and cultural lines in the classic American novel, the other two pairs being Ishmael and the Polynesian Queequeg in Melville's *Moby Dick* and Huck and the Negro slave Jim in Mark Twain's *Huckleberry Finn* – white and red, white and brown and, finally, white and black. The most insightful thing about this relationship was said by D.H. Lawrence when he observed:

> What did Cooper dream beyond democracy? Why, in his immortal friendship of Chingachgook and Natty Bumppo he dreamed the nucleus of a new society. That is, he dreamed a new human relationship. . . . This is the new nucleus of a new society, the clue to a new world-epoch.
>
> (78)

Turning finally to the Indian novel, let me begin by saying that the situation here is like that in Russia and unlike that in America in the existence of a long national or native past. But let me immediately mention the differences. The most important for us in India is that (a) the West was not an external point of reference but a long imperialist presence and power which made the modern/ancient, native/foreign, East/West polarity that much more compelling and conflictual, and (b) the use and spread of the English language over and above our own languages in itself highlighted the polarities in our national self-consciousness. Overall, however, in the definition of nationality, the same attitudes operate as in Russia: either turning inward or backward or outward and westward, or defining our nationality in terms of both the native past as well as the modern West.

The novel in India emerges under this two-way pressure in the later part of the 19th and early 20th century in several languages at more or less the same time. The most interesting material for the present context might be provided by the 'Indian language' novels, but having little competence in this area, I shall confine myself to the Indian novel written in English, in fact, to just one old-fashioned novelist; in fact, even there, to just one common aspect of the many novels he wrote.

We all know of Fredric Jameson's thesis that all Third World novels must be, inevitably, 'national allegories'. We also know of Aijaz Ahmed's critique of this thesis in his book *In Theory*, subtitled *Nations, Classes, Literatures*, and his demonstration that all Third World novels neither need be, inevitably, nor in fact are anything like 'national allegories'.[14] While this is true and convincingly proved by Aijaz Ahmed with detailed reference to the Urdu tradition, quite a few Indian novels written in English can in fact be viewed in Jameson's terms. Salman Rushdie's *Midnight's Children* is a narcissistic-allegorical-journalistic-historical novel that depicts Indianness as a hugely comic combination or confusion of the East and the West, the native and the colonized.

In *Imaginary Homelands*, Rushdie describes his position as a 'transnational subject':

> It may be that writers in my position, exiles or emigrants or expatriates, are haunted by some sense of loss, some urge to reclaim, to look back. . . . But if we do look back we must also do so in the knowledge . . . that our physical alienation from India almost inevitably means that we will not be capable of reclaiming precisely the thing that was lost; that we will, in short, create fictions, not actual cities or villages, but invisible ones, imaginary homelands, Indias of the mind.
>
> (10)

Tim Brennan critiques the 'creative duplicity' of 'cosmopolitan writers of the Third World' like Rushdie (30–1) whose literary devices, 'allusion, metaphor, allegory and parable, are all like nationalism itself, "janus-faced" ', with one face toward the West (34). *Midnight's Children* is an allegorical history of modern India, Saleem Sinai's personal history paralleling the history of the independent nation. It uses fable and fabulation and what has been called a 'chutnification' of myth and reality and at the linguistic level of Hindustani and English, 'Indian English', something not used by older novelists such as R.K. Narayan.

Narayan deals neither in fashionable modes of fiction-writing nor in themes of eye-catching topicality. In his ten novels he insists on matters of everyday life in Malgudi, the fictional world he has created, but through which he explores an important theme, a theme of all modern history, society, politics and, directly or indirectly, overtly or implicitly, all modern Indian literature as well – the theme of the East and the West. Behind Malgudi, in Graham Greene's words in his Introduction to *The Bachelor of Arts*, 'we are aware, not of an individual author . . . but of a whole national condition' (ix). Not certainly the *whole* national condition, but I would say the most appropriate part of it in terms of the *comic* confusion of the native and the foreign. Actually, the West is non-existent in Narayan except for *The Vendor of Sweets* and the last scene of *The Guide*. In the bulk of his fiction it is only the East, but, far from eschewing this important theme in modern Indian history, Narayan shows us what it truly means not to this or that individual, but to a considerable section of Indian society striving to live its daily life in a definite historical situation.

He takes the point that is really important in the equation, India, seeing that for a sizeable and static portion of Indian society the social and cultural impingement in the other direction has been negligible. There is little room in the Malgudi novels for any English characters – one can think only of the marginal Brown, the Principal of the local mission college, and the still more marginal company director in *Mr. Sampath*; there are no 'bridge parties'; in these novels, as in colonial India, Englishmen are talked about rather than talked to by the vast majority of Indians. In the matter of language and dialogue, Narayan does not use 'Indian English', the Indian accent or 'Indianisms' for comic effect, and the English language is a neutral instrument through which he expresses not only the general Indian sensibility but a whole range of character, personality and temperament.

Narayan in *Next Sunday* describes his hero as 'the modern unknown warrior, who is the middle-class common man' ('On Humour', 54), the same as his cartoonist brother Laxman's Common Man. It is true in that his novels project middle-class characters but there are hardly any heroes. Malgudi itself is the central representation of the Malgudi novels. And what is the great corporate literary creation called Malgudi? Why should it be Malgudi rather than Madras or Bombay? Just as Wessex, made famous in Thomas Hardy's fiction, is the microcosm of the declining English agricultural community, and Yoknapatawpha County made famous in William Faulkner's novels that of the declining and decadent southern 'aristocracy' of the United States, each involving a sense of tragedy on the part of their respective authors, Malgudi is an Indian small town situated at a nicely calculated comic distance between the East and the West. For the Indian villages, though ravaged by colonial exploitation, were relatively untouched, socially and culturally, by the impact of the English, while the large metropolitan centres tended to be much too thoroughly Westernized. The Indian small town, Malgudi, is for

Narayan's purpose, the perfect comic product or by-product of the British colonial presence in India.

Narayan's purpose is to show its influence everywhere on the surface of life and, at the same time, its inability to penetrate deeply anywhere to life's essentials including civil and family relations. Malgudi, in its mixture of East and West, is both a concrete individual place and at the same time representative of a general social condition. While being itself faithfully, it is also any Indian small town. On the one hand, the cramped older quarters of the town, and adjacent to them the Lawley and New Extensions, what elsewhere may be the Civil Lines or the Model Town, with their bungalows and garden homes and imitated Western style of living. Equally familiar is the statue of some forgotten British administrator associated by the natives with a legendary hero of their own. Here is the Select Picture House and the Regal Haircutting Saloon, the co-operative society or bank meant to benefit the very peasantry that distrusts it most, the town municipality that punctually surveys the town gutter at election time and, as punctually after the elections are over, abandons it to its time-honoured ways. And here, above all, is cricket, and not only cricket, but the M.C.C., standing both for the Malgudi and the Marylebone Cricket Clubs, associated in the minds of schoolboys with the far-off glamour of English and Australian stars while playing at street corners with improvised stumps and boundary lines made of chalk.

Much of the emphasis in Narayan falls on education which, after all, was the chief means of Western impingement on traditional Indian life. Thus we have a central place given to the Mission School and the Mission College with a curriculum that includes *Othello* and Charles Lamb and Milton. A native poet, in fact, seeks to outrival Milton by composing an epic on Krishna's life but strictly, for some reason, in monosyllabic verse: 'Girls with girls did dance in trance' (*The Man-Eater of Malgudi*, Ch. 1, 5)! And since education is seen only as a means to the acquisition of a degree, never as anything of value in itself, the emphasis is on the crucial importance of examinations, their doomsday character. The degree in its turn is important marginally because it gives status, but mainly because it opens the way to a job or profession, 'earning money' or simply 'earning'.

The Malgudi novels, like those that constitute the main body of English fiction, are concerned with the middle class, but what makes Narayan different is that his concern is with the unique cultural character of that class – the Indian middle class of the last century or so, which would certainly not have come to possess its peculiar identity without the influence of British presence and polity, above all the influence of British educational policy. The mission school boys, the Bachelor of Arts, the English teacher, the printers and editors of English weeklies, the railway stallholder and guide, even a comic Gandhian satyagrahi such as the aging hero of *The Vendor of Sweets*, not to mention the vast army of English-knowing clerks in the background – these would simply not have come into existence except for the impact of the British, they are types thrown up by the mad, comic mixing of the East and the West, and the comedy lies in the mixture.

It is a mistake, I think, to regard personal relations as Narayan's theme. That is a recent Western preoccupation inspired by the human situation in Western society. Narayan is an Indian or old-fashioned writer in the sense that he writes of an older world. In this world communication and relations are in no way a problem. Social and personal relations are rather something that surround us like the atmosphere, not wholly pure, sometimes quite polluted, but given, necessary, inescapable, something that is the condition of one's existence but about which one thinks as little as about the air one breathes. Likewise, though Narayan is far from sentimentalizing the idea of continuity, it too constitutes a value of his comedy. Beneath the surface, Malgudi remains the relatively untouched 'natio', tradition-bound, living within the framework of ancient customs, resistant to change, static if not stagnant. Graham Greene recognizes this when he says in his Introduction to *The Financial Expert*, 'the life of Malgudi – never ruffled by politics – proceeds in exactly the same way as it has done for centuries, and the juxtaposition of the age-old convention and the modern character provides much of the comedy' (vii). Malgudi is thus a continuous social fabric, in space and time, testifying to the continuity of social life rather than personal survival. And it is because Narayan sees these facts – community, communication and continuity – at the base of social life that he can still write recognizable (if old-fashioned) comedy rather than the sort of comedy – tragi-comedy, grim comedy, the comedy of the absurd, whatever the name – written by Western novelists and playwrights who see in life only isolation, incommunication and disjunction.

Narayan is an Indian writer writing in English, but with a clear sense of his identity and the national boundaries within which and about which he is writing. More recently, the Indian writers in English describe themselves as transnational as Rushdie does, and Bharati Mukherjee, for instance, announces the end of nationality when she states in *The Lady from Lucknow*: 'The traveller feels at home everywhere, because she is never at home anywhere' (31). More famously, so does Amitav Ghosh, whose *The Shadow Lines* sees nationality not even as an invention but as an illusion. The novel, according to the blurb, focuses on 'nationalism, the Shadow Line we draw between people and nations, which is both an absurd illusion and a source of terrifying violence' (298). Amitav Ghosh recognizes no separate or cultural realities that deserve to be recognized. For him, all such demarcations are shadow lines, arbitrary and invented divisions.

Both the writers I have mentioned are, of course, expatriates like so many other Indian writers writing in English today, with frequent and easy access across national borders, shadow lines indeed for them. For them, globalization or transnationalism is the answer. Does this then signal the end of nationality as a literary theme, or does this apply only to the Indian novelists who write in English? All I can say by way of conclusion is that I find it rather astonishing that, in a gymnastic feat of high calibre, the Indian novel in English should, in the space of one generation, have moved from the struggle to define the national condition to the freewheeling exposition of what Zbigniew Brzezinski, National Security Advisor to President Jimmy Carter, called 'a new planetary consciousness'.[15]

Notes

1 Nikolai Shelgunov (1824–91), a revolutionary democrat, journalist and literary critic, and Mikhail Mikhailov (1827–65), writer of fiction, radical political sympathizer and advocate of reform, co-authored *The Young Generation*, one of the most important manifestos to be written, which advocated change and broke with czarism. It was printed in London by Herzen (1812–70), 'the father of Russian socialism'. Both Shelgunov and Mikhailov were arrested and exiled.

2 Czar Nicholas I, who reigned from 1825 to 1855, was an autocrat and a reactionary who propagated the three principles of 'orthodoxy, autocracy and nationality'. His son and successor, Alexander II (1855–81), enacted the most significant reform, the emancipation of the serfs, in 1861 and earned the title 'Alexander the Liberator'.

3 A secret revolutionary movement in the first quarter of the 19th century in Russia culminated in an unsuccessful revolt in St. Petersburg on December 26, 1825, hence the name. Russian army officers led 3000 soldiers in protest against Czar Nicholas I, who assumed the throne when his brother Constantine married a plebeian Polish woman and opted out of the line of succession.

4 Alexander Sergeyevich Pushkin (1799–1837), poet, novelist, dramatist, short-story writer, is considered the founder of modern Russian literature and Russia's greatest poet. *Eugene Onegin* (1833), written under the influence of Byron, presents a panoramic view of Russian life. Pushkin was killed in a duel in 1837 (as was Lermontov in 1841).

5 Mikhail Evgrafovich Saltykov-Shchedrin (1826–89) was a major Russian humorist and satirist, a zealous promoter of reforms, whose best-known work is *The Golovlyov Family*.

6 Pechorin, the main character in Mikhail Lermontov's *A Hero of Our Time* (1840), Beltov in Alexander Herzen's *Who Is to Blame?* (1845–6) and Rudin in Ivan Turgenev's novel of the same name (1856) are all, like Eugene Onegin, 'superfluous men'. Turgenev wrote a novella, *The Diary of a Superfluous Man*, in 1850, and the term was applied retrospectively to these characters, who were talented, capable individuals but indifferent to society and to other human beings, unambitious, cynical, bored, occupying themselves drinking, gambling, duelling – in short, wasting their lives.

7 Vissarion Grigoryevich Belinsky (1811–48), the most gifted and formidable
   Russian critic of the 19th century, laid the foundation of Russian literary criticism and was the father of Russian radical intelligentsia. He believed that art
   and the history of a nation were closely connected and that Russian literature
   could help the Russian nation to develop and mature. He praised writers like
   Pushkin (on whom he published eleven articles), Gogol, Lermontov, Dostoevsky, Turgenev and Goncharov and argued that art should be judged for social
   as well as aesthetic qualities.

   Nikolay Aleksandrovich Dobrolyubov (1836–61), poet, journalist and revolutionary democrat, was the most influential literary critic after Belinsky, and his
   contribution to literary theory was the addition of 'social types'. His fame rests
   on four essays, among them 'What is Oblomovitis?', an analysis of the character
   of Oblomov in Goncharov's novel, which established the term 'Oblomovism' as
   a name for the superfluous man of Russian life and literature, peculiar to Russia,
   the by-product of serfdom.

8 Pavel Vasilyevich Annenkov (1813–87), Russian critic, memoirist and friend
   of authors and literary critics, reproduces these words as Belinsky's but without
   quotation marks in his literary memoirs, *The Extraordinary Decade,* published
   in 1880 (218). Joe Andrew in *Writers and Society during the Rise of Russian
   Realism,* citing Annenkov, repeats them but in quotation marks (146).

9 Nikolai Vasilievich Gogol (1809–52), Russian dramatist of Ukrainian origin
   and satirist, the author of *Dead Souls* (1842), was a preeminent figure in the
   foundation of Russian realism and much admired by Pushkin and Belinsky.
   Dead Souls is a picture of feudal Russia, and Chichikov is a swindler who wants
   to get rich quickly, the political corruption and abuses being castigated through
   laughter and satire.

10 Ivan Alexandrovich Goncharov (1812–91), who served in many official capaci-
   ties including that of literary censor, is best known for his novels, *A Common
   Story* (1847), his masterpiece *Oblomov* (1859) and *The Precipice* (1869). Dostoevsky and Chekhov praised him very highly.

   Dmitri Ivan Pisarev (1840–68), radical writer and social critic, arrested for
   his anti-government writings and imprisoned until 1866, attacked Pushkin's
   Onegin but praised Goncharov's *Oblomov.* In the year in which Goncharov's
   novel appeared, he published an article entitled 'Oblomov' in *Rassvet* (St.
   Petersburg) 10 (1859), 5–21, and since it is a full examination of *Oblomov* it
   can be assumed that the quotation in the text is from this piece and not from
   Pisarev's 1861 article on Pisemsky, Turgenev and Goncharov. The 1859 article
   is listed by Amy Singleton in *Noplace Like Home,* Chapter 4, Note 4, 163. I am
   grateful to Ahmer Anwer for providing the reference.

11 'The Land of Cockaigne', a French poem from the 13th century, describes a
   land of milk and honey, a land of plenty and harmony and sensual pleasure. An
   English poem of the same name written in the early to mid-14th century by a
   Franciscan friar satirizes the life of monks.

12 Hector St. John de Crevecoeur (1735–1813), born into a French noble family, who emigrated to America in 1755 and was naturalized in New York as
   John Hector St. John, was a French-American writer. He served in the French
   and Indian War and, following the defeat of the French Army (by the British),
   moved to New York, bought a farm and worked as a farmer. In 1782 he published the essays entitled *Letters from an American Farmer,* a great literary success in Europe. He was the first writer to describe life on the American frontier

and the concept of the 'American Dream' and to create an American identity. At the end of his life he returned to France and died there.
13 The four other novels in the Leatherstocking series following *The Pioneers* are *The Last of the Mohicans* (1826), *The Prairie* (1827), *The Pathfinder* (1840) and *The Deerslayer* (1841).
14 Fredric Jameson published his theory in an article, 'Third World Literature in the Age of Multinationalism', in *Social Text*, Fall 1986, and Aijaz Ahmed replied with 'Jameson's Rhetoric of Otherness and the National Allegory' also in *Social Text*, Fall 1987 (later included in his book *In Theory*).
15 The Belgian communications scholar Armand Mattelart supports the one-world thesis of Marx and Engels and the transformation of national and local literatures into a single world literature. The 'transnationalization process', in Mattelart's words, 'creates . . . to use the terms of Brzezinski, "a new planetary consciousness", a new "harmony", a "new world unity" and a new "consensus"' (57).

Works cited

General

Anderson, Benedict. *Imagined Communities: Reflections on the Origins and Spread of Nationalism*. London and New York: Verso, 1983.
Brennan, Timothy. *Salman Rushdie and the Third World: Myths of the Nation*. Houndmills and Basingstoke, Hampshire: Macmillan, 1989.
Chatterjee, Partha. "Whose Imagined Community?". *The Nation and its Fragments: Colonial and Postcolonial Histories. The Partha Chatterjee Omnibus*. Delhi: Oxford University Press, 1999.
Gellner, Ernest. *Thought and Change*. London: Weidenfeld and Nicholson, 1964.
Ricoeur, Paul. 'Civilization and National Cultures'. *History and Truth*. Evanston, IL: Northwestern University Press, 1965.
Shakespeare, William. *A Midsummer Night's Dream*. Ed. Norman Sanders. Basingstoke and London: Macmillan, 1971.
Williams, Raymond. 'The Culture of Nations'. *Towards 2000*. London: Chatto & Windus, 1983.

The English novel

Austen, Jane. *Emma*. Introduction by Lionel Trilling. Boston: Houghton Mifflin Company, 1957.
Tocqueville, Alexis de. *The Old Regime and the French Revolution*. Tr. Stuart Gilbert. New York: Doubleday, 1955.
Trilling, Lionel. *Introduction to Jane Austen's Emma*. Boston: Houghton Mifflin Company, 1957.

The Russian novel

Andrew, Joe. *Writers and Society During the Rise of Russian Realism*. London: Macmillan, 1980.

Annenkov, Pavel V. *The Extraordinary Decade: Literary Memoirs*. Ed. Arthur P. Mendel. Tr. Irwin R. Titunik. Ann Arbor: The University of Michigan Press, 1968.

Bayley, John. 'Introduction'. *Eugene Onegin*. Tr. Charles Johnston. London: Penguin Books, 1977.

Belinsky, Vissarion G. *Selected Philosophical Works*. Moscow: Foreign Languages Publishing House, 1956.

Dobrolyubov, Nikolai A. *Belinsky, Chernyshevsky and Dobrolyubov: Selected Criticism*. Ed. Ralph E. Matlaw. Bloomington and London: Indiana University Press, 1976.

Dostoevsky, Fyodor M. 'Tribute to George Sand, June 1876'. *The Diary of a Writer*. Tr. and Annotated by Boris Brasol. New York: George Brasilier, 1954.

Frank, Joseph. *Dostoevsky: A Writer in His Time*. Princeton and Oxford: Princeton University Press, 2010.

Freeborn, Richard. *The Rise of the Russian Novel: Studies in the Russian Novel from Eugene Onegin to War and Peace*. Cambridge: Cambridge University Press, 1973.

Goncharov, Ivan A. *Oblomov*. Tr. and with an Introduction. David Magarshack. London: Penguin Books, 1954.

Pisarev, Dmitri I. 'Oblomov'. *Rassvet* (St. Petersburg), 10 (1859), 5–21. Listed in Amy C. Singleton. *Noplace Like Home: The Literary Artist and Russia's Search for Cultural Identity*. Albany: State University of New York Press, 1997.

Pushkin, Alexander S. *Eugene Onegin*. Tr. Charles Johnston. Introduction John Bayley. London: Penguin Books, 1977.

Saltykov-Shchedrin, Mikhail E. *The Golovlyov Family*. London: J.M. Dent and Sons Ltd., 1934.

Shelgunov, Nikolai V. and Mikhail L. Mikhailov. *To the Young Generation*. Quoted in Joseph Frank *Dostoevsky: A Writer in His Time*, pp. 332–35.

Tennyson, Alfred Lord. 'The Lotos Eaters'. *Poems of Tennyson*. With an Introduction by T. Herbert Warren. London: Oxford University Press, 1910.

The American novel

Brady, Charles A. 'James Fenimore Cooper: Myth-Maker and Christian Romancer'. *American Classics Reconsidered*. Ed. Harold C. Gardiner. New York: Scribner's, 1958.

Cooper, James Fenimore. *New York*. Ed. Dixon Ryan Fox. New York: William Farquhar Payson, 1930.

———. *The Pioneers*. Introduction Donald A. Ringe. New York and London: Penguin Books, 1988.

Crevecoeur, Hector St. John. *Letters from an American Farmer*. Ed. with an Introduction. Dennis D. Moore. Cambridge: Belknap Press of Harvard University Press, 2013.

Emerson, Ralph Waldo. 'The American Scholar'. *The Complete Writings of Ralph Waldo Emerson*. 2 Vols. New York: W.H. Wise & Co., 1929, Vol. 1, pp. 25–36.

James, Henry. *Selected Letters*. Ed. Leon Edel. Cambridge: Belknap Press of Harvard University Press, 1987.
Lawrence, D.H. *Studies in Classic American Literature*. New York: Thomas Seltzer, 1923.
Whitman, Walt. *Song of Myself. Complete Poetry and Collected Prose*. New York, NY: Literary Classics of the United States, 1982.

The Indian novel

Ahmed, Aijaz. 'Jameson's Rhetoric of Otherness and the "National Allegory"'. *In Theory: Classes, Nations, Literatures*. London and New York: Verso, 1992.
Brennan, Timothy. *Salman Rushdie and the Third World: Myths of the Nation*. Houndmills and Basingstoke, Hampshire: Macmillan, 1989.
Ghosh, Amitav. *The Shadow Lines*. Delhi: Oxford University Press, 1995.
Greene, Graham. *Introduction to The Bachelor of Arts*. London: Thomas Nelson and Sons Ltd., 1937.
———. *Introduction to The Financial Expert*. London: Methuen, 1952.
Jameson, Frederic. 'Third World Literature in the Age of Multinationalism'. *Social Text*, Fall 1986, pp. 65–88.
Mattelart, Armand and Seth Siegelaub. Eds. 'Introduction'. *Communications and Class Struggle*, 2 Vols. New York: International General, 1983, Vol. 2.
Mukherjee, Bharati. 'The Lady from Lucknow'. *Darkness*. Markham, ON: Penguin Books Canada, 1985, pp. 23–34.
Narayan, R.K. *The Bachelor of Arts*. Introduction by Graham Greene. London: Thomas Nelson and Sons Ltd., 1937.
———. *The Financial Expert*. Introduction by Graham Greene. London: Methuen, 1952.
———. *Swami and Friends*. East Lansing: Michigan State College Press, 1954.
———. *The English Teacher*. Mysore: Indian Thought Publications, 1955.
———. *Mr. Sampath*. Mysore: Indian Thought Publications, 1956.
———. *Next Sunday*. Bombay: Pearl Publications, 1960.
———. *The Man-Eater of Malgudi*. London: Four Square, 1965.
———. *The Vendor of Sweets*. New York: Viking Press, 1967.
———. *The Guide*. New York: Penguin Books, 2006.
Rushdie, Salman. *Midnight's Children*. London: Jonathan Cape, 1981.
———. *Imaginary Homelands: Essays and Criticism 1981–1991*. London: Granta Books, 1991.

3 Ideology and the novel

Today I shall focus again on a few well-known, old-fashioned, 19th-century American novels, usually called 'romances', to illustrate from a different point of view and in yet another theoretical context, the manner in which the polarities of the private and the public, the individual and the social, operate within these novels. Needless to add that for this context, as for the others I have used, other texts could be considered instead of the ones I have chosen, but the ones I shall discuss seem to me to demonstrate most incisively the argument I shall advance with regard to ideology and the novel.

I wish I could at this point proceed straightaway to the novels and let them speak for themselves, but, as before, there is first this question of ideology itself which is more complicated a question than 'nationalism' or the 'epic'. Mr. Chairperson, a moment ago you used the word 'comprehensive'. The word that comes to my mind when I read people is the word 'comprehensible', and I would sacrifice 'comprehensiveness' for 'comprehensibility'. And that is what I am trying to do in coming to terms with ideology.

There is no doubt that the theory and concept of ideology as developed from Marx to Althusser and beyond does represent a good and relevant way of studying societies that tend to maintain their relations of power and domination, not so much through coercion and repression unless necessary as a last resort – I cannot think of any society, any Western country, which will not go back to naked repression when necessary – but which generally try to maintain their relations of power and domination through common consent or 'hegemony', as Gramsci might put it.

Ideological analysis thus, it may be said in a preliminary way, explores precisely this unrecognized but nevertheless deep and pervasive connection between the subjective and the political, the inner and the outer, what seems natural and self-evidently true but is, in fact, socially constructed – in short, the very constitution of the 'free' individual through subjection to social necessity and material determinism. But, while I am convinced that this is a useful concept for the study of society and literature, so much has been written on it, that ideology itself – as term, concept, theory – has become vexed in recent times, and anyone using it must explain it as clearly as possible.

A great deal of literature has accumulated on the subject in several, almost all disciplines, in which, however, there is little perspectival or even conceptual agreement. It has been said that there are as many theories of ideology as there are theorists of it. In Althusser himself, Adam Schaff,[1] the renowned Polish Jewish philosopher and semiotician, counts ten definitions of ideology, not all of them compatible with each other, not to mention two divergent views with altogether different implications.

This being so, I must clarify my own view of the concept, my view of its usefulness in the analysis of literary texts, and, in due course, my fundamental disagreement with a whole line of influential literary critics who have used this concept, beginning with Pierre Macherey, to, my texts being American, the leaders of the American school of ideological critics, namely, Professors Sacvan Bercovitch and Myra Jehlen.

What do I mean by Ideology? I think, to begin with, I have to rehearse things that may even be obvious. First, negatively, what I do not mean – as the Vedas say, a 'Neti, Neti' ('Not This, Not This') sort of enumeration. Not, of course, ideology in common parlance as a systematic set of beliefs or political doctrine such as socialist ideology or Hindutva. Nor in its original sense in the writer who coined the term, the early 19th-century French Enlightenment writer, Destutt de Tracy,[2] for whom Ideology was like, say, biology, and meant a scientific study of ideas. And not, above all for me, ideology as a normative concept, a phenomenon universal to all societies, a paradigm of belief and value systems necessary for social cohesion, as in Max Weber[3] and Parsonian Functionalism[4] – there can be no society without a paradigmatic set of belief systems, values, because this (normative concept) is always there and always necessary.

This is one of the two divergent views of ideology in Althusser's writings,[5] what he calls 'ideology *in general*' (*Lenin and Philosophy*, 150), which he says '*hails or interpellates concrete individuals as concrete subjects*' (*Lenin and Philosophy*, 162), something not only 'profoundly', that is to say, inaccessibly, '*unconscious*' (*For Marx*, 233), but also '*eternal, exactly like the unconscious*' (*Lenin and Philosophy*, 152). To the extent that this view of 'ideology in general' in Althusser sees it as social cement, 'profoundly unconscious', I have no further use for it because, according to me, if there is anything of value to be found in the concept of ideology, it is to be found in the critical rather than the normative concept of it. As Anthony Giddens puts it: '*the chief usefulness of the concept of ideology concerns the critique of domination*', enabling us to see '*how structures of signification are mobilised to legitimate the sectional interests of hegemonic groups'* (187–8).

As a critical concept, ideology originates in Marx, *The German Ideology* as well as his later writings, goes through hints in other writers, especially Gramsci, and culminates in Althusser, mainly in the attention-drawing, famous/infamous essay, 'Ideology and Ideological State Apparatuses'. I do not wish to go into the internal debates within this broadly Marxist tradition, much less into the endless polemics of the scholars of this tradition from the time of Althusser. I would rather define the main, broad points that emerge from these writings, referring first to a quarrel which is, in fact, no quarrel at all, namely, the quarrel between the cognitive and the materialist views of ideology.

The cognitive theory may be said to be as old as Bacon's 'idols' or false ideas, errors of cognition that science, rationality, would rectify, or Destutt de Tracy whose whole enterprise was the rational, scientific, elimination of prejudice. The theory became critical precisely when Marx linked these miscognitions, distortions, inversions and, indeed, the whole consciousness of human beings to the material conditions of life – not only the famous sentence in the Preface to *A Contribution to the Critique of Political Economy*, 'It is not the consciousness of men that determines their existence but, on the contrary, their social existence determines their consciousness' (11–12), but even in *The German Ideology*: 'Life is not determined by consciousness but consciousness by life' (15). Or, 'The ideas of the ruling class are in every epoch the ruling ideas: i.e. the class, which is the ruling *material* force of society, is at the same time its ruling *intellectual* force' (39).

Thus, broadly speaking, the two, to my mind, for clarity, essential components of Ideology are: (a) the inner, the psychological – the miscognitions, the distortions, in and of the consciousness and, crucially for the critical concept; (b) their connection with the material interests of the dominant class or group. The two are not mutually exclusive inasmuch as one relates to ideology's area of operation and the other to its origin. Trying to work this out, I was reminded of Wordsworth's definition of 'poetry' as 'the spontaneous overflow of powerful feelings: it takes its origin from emotion recollected in tranquillity' (Preface to the *Lyrical Ballads*, 1802, 173). This seems a contradictory statement until we realize that Wordsworth is not saying that poetry is the one *and* the other. It is 'the spontaneous overflow of powerful feelings' and it 'takes its origin from emotion recollected in tranquillity'. So that I might say that while ideology functions within us powerfully as cognitions or miscognitions, feelings, it takes its origin from what is outside, the material and social conditions of existence in any epoch. It is precisely in this sense that Gramsci – best known for his theory of cultural hegemony and whose *Prison Notebooks* are considered a highly original contribution to 20th-century political theory – makes his famous distinction between arbitrary and 'historically organic'. In his words, ideologies are, rightly speaking, not arbitrary but 'historically organic' – that is, 'necessary to a given structure'. He goes on: 'historically necessary, they have a validity which is "psychological", they "organize" human masses, and create the terrain on which men . . . acquire consciousness' (376–7).

Coming to Althusser, his merit, his originality, thus, does not lie so much in underlining, in pointing out the material existence of ideology. His originality in this respect has been much exaggerated. I think, the merit, at least for me, of Althusser and his followers lies rather in what I call the crucial elaborations, the demonstration of (a) the pervasiveness and (b) the penetration of ideology's operations in modern societies. On the one hand, his identification of various 'Ideological State Apparatuses' – an unfortunate phrase which he himself was not prepared to defend and even abandoned, a more accurate phrase being institutional matrices of ideology, such as Family, Education, Church, Religion (which can hardly be called State Apparatuses), but pointing to these, a whole range of institutional matrices of ideology and, beyond these, a whole range of cultural practices and signifying systems at one end, horizontally, the pervasiveness. More important, at the other end, the penetration of ideology's operations within human consciousness or subjectivity, so that it is no longer a matter of ideas or ideas only, but something deeper than ideas, something that shapes and structures our ideas as well as our values, our feelings, our very perceptions, from even sensory perceptions to the perceptions of signs including linguistic signs. Ideology, one may thus say, is like the air which surrounds us on all sides, which we breathe constantly but which we ordinarily never notice – unless suffocated!

What I have outlined from my reading of other people is, I do think, a true picture of how ideology pervades us from all sides in our ordinary daily lives. But think here, for a moment, of how complete a scenario this is for the novelist who, by focussing on the daily inner and outer life of a single individual can, through that focussing, thus achieve a critique not just of intermediary institutions such as the family, but get in touch with, more importantly, a critique of the material social structure itself. That some classic novelists, in fact, do precisely this is what I will try to show later, novelists who may be called pre-Althusser Althusserians.

But here I must suggest the obvious, most crippling aspect of Althusser's theory of ideology, which has crippled so many literary critics as well, including chiefly the leaders of the American school of ideological criticism. To simplify, I would call this crippling aspect an ironclad ideological determinism, ideology as a cradle-to-grave prisonhouse, from which there is no escape, from which no break is possible through any means whatsoever as far as Bercovitch and many culture critics are concerned. For Althusser himself, the break can come only through 'science', by which he means abstract theory. I think this begs the question of where 'science' itself is to come from. If science can put to flight, can dispel, ideology, what is the origin of science itself? Besides the point that science also can become ideological as Jürgen Habermas (associated with the Frankfurt School) has argued in 'Technology and Science as Ideology' in *Toward a Rational Society*. The truth is, that in his challenge to humanism and historicism, Althusser insists on the ideological construction of the subject to the point where the human subject and human agency simply disappear.

I will not enter into the theory-praxis debate here but will instead make two citations to clarify my own point of view. First, Marx in *The German Ideology* – early Marx, pre-epistemology-break Marx – where he says that the 'practical dissolution' of ideological notions, inversions, distortions, their 'removal . . . from the consciousness of man, will . . . be effected by altered circumstances, not by theoretical deductions' (31–2). The 'altered circumstances' that dissolve or dispel ideology need not be in themselves revolutionary in character. They can be social or personal crises of other kinds, including, as E.P. Thompson says in his polemical essay against Althusser ('The Poverty of Theory'), very apropos to the novels I am discussing today:

> crises of subsistence, trench warfare, unemployment, inflation, genocide. People are imprisoned: in prison they meditate in new ways about the law. [Cf. Hester Prynne or even Huck Finn especially on the raft.] In the face of such general experiences, old conceptual systems may crumble and new problematics insist upon their presence.
>
> (9)

Experience in this sense, as the junction between social being and consciousness, is Thompson's central category in his argument with Althusser about the re-entry of the subject into history and the nature of the historical process as against structure in general. But here I would emphasize the first step, the destabilization of the ideologically constructed subject and the crumbling of ideology which Thompson calls 'old conceptual systems', under the pressure of experience, defined, not just as events and happenings, but the critical interplay *between* happenings and consciousness.

The novels I discuss today – Melville's *Benito Cereno*, Twain's *Huckleberry Finn* and Hawthorne's *The Scarlet Letter* – can all be called novels of experience in this sense and this is the process in them I shall highlight, beginning by citing a novelist's, Henry James's, definition of 'Experience' in his Preface to the *Princess Casamassima*, to parallel that of the historian Thompson: 'Experience, as I see it, is our apprehension and our measure of what happens to us as social creatures – any intelligent report of which has to be based on that apprehension' (Vol. 1, xii).

A moment ago I said that the novels I am discussing can be called novels of experience with the focus on the junction point between social being and consciousness, but now I can say that they can be called intelligent reports, to use James's phrase, 'our apprehension and our measure of what happens to us as social creatures – any intelligent report of which has to be based on that apprehension'.

Now, before coming to these 'intelligent reports' and dealing with them individually, let me say, as a general preface, these being my views regarding ideology, in my discussion of the novels that follow:

a First of all, my reading of them has nothing to do with that 'symptomatic' reading of ideological critics like Pierre Macherey – a student of Althusser's and a central figure in the development of French post-structuralism and Marxism – who, in a sort of Freudianism underlying even Althusser's own notion that ideology is 'profoundly unconscious', look for the text's deeply concealed ideology in, not what it says, but in its 'gaps and absences', its 'significant silences' (Translator's Preface, viii).

   Least of all do I agree with such sleuthing when practiced by Professors Sacvan Bercovitch and Myra Jehlen on the American classic texts of the 19th century, leading to the discovery that the ideology all these texts conceal is what they call 'middle-class' ideology since the 'nineteenth-century novel is quintessentially the genre of the middle class' (125), a loose term but in no way applicable to novels that have little to do with the middle class or with love and marriage, and whose heroes are marginal or marginalized characters, standing, often, in opposition to, if not in repudiation of, family, school, church and the whole system of bourgeois property relations.

b So far from the idea that literary texts being the 'products of ideology' in all cases cannot 'know' ideology, being creatures of ideology themselves, I would say of the American classics what Jonathan Dollimore says of the English Renaissance writers in *Radical Tragedy*, namely, that they 'possessed a sophisticated concept of ideology if not the word' (18).

c Further, in the case of the American writers, they not only understood ideology's relation to material interest and power, one of the two components, but also its interior operations at the level of values, feelings, perceptions – perceptions of the world, self, the other, as well as of signs, including, I repeat, those linguistic signs that constitute the key words of culture.

d   Further still, not merely do they *know* ideology, but what they do in fact to some extent is make their characters recognize it, interrogate it, destabilize it, overthrow it and even subvert it.

e   One last point: the ideology concerned here in these three novels relates to three main issues – race, gender, class – the three main areas of social repression. When I say 'class', it is not class consciousness in the sense in which we understand it today but what Gramsci describes as 'merely . . . the first glimmer of such consciousness, in other words, merely . . . the basic negative, polemical attitude' (273). However momentarily, contra ideology, some of these characters develop this kind of class consciousness, a counter consciousness of their own, which is not fully articulated as such, but, in Gramsci's way of thinking, the pre-consciousness of class consciousness.

One other prefatory remark beginning as before – as promised and as bound by my sub-title – with the novelists's own definition: what did the novelists think of what they were doing? Some of these novels have been called 'Romances' by the writers themselves: Hawthorne in his Prefaces, no doubt, called his novels 'romances', in one of them, the Dedicatory Letter to the 'Snow-Image', describing himself as 'burrowing, to his utmost ability, into the depths of our common nature, for the purposes of psychological romance' (xx). But much more by a whole generation of critics who wrote, in fact, during the years of the Cold War and, I may add, the American political climate of those years, and built a whole theory of the American novel as 'Romance'.

I do not wish to enter into this question of the American Romance versus the European novel at the level of theory. I will only remind you that we are back at the polarity of the socio-historical on the one hand, and, on the other, the moral-universal – expanded now to include the American novel. We are back, in other words, to the same old story – human nature, pride, vanity, something called 'common nature', the truths of the human heart, original sin – and I must warn you about what ground I will take with which you must be familiar by now. I will make, therefore, only one general statement in this context and give one illustration of how I view these novels in contradistinction to how the romance theorists view them.

I have no objection at all to calling the American novel 'Romance' – labels are not important – provided one does not thereby lose sight of its central, social, critical function. Provided, that is, one views it as (if I may have the luxury of quoting myself for once),

a mode of writing which involves the strategy of breaking away from reality and realism in order to subject them – that is, both 19th century socio-historical reality and its appropriate socio-historical mode of representation – to a critique from alien and alienating points of view or vantage.

(7–8)

To support this statement I shall not invoke their bringing in of alien cultures such as the American Indian in Cooper or the Polynesian in Melville or the utopian socialist experiment in Hawthorne's *Blithedale Romance*, and how much they are brought in to provide a point of view or vantage from an alien culture reflecting upon the culture that is doing the reflecting, what Blithedale tells us about Boston and Boston about Blithedale. I will only refer to one romance feature of these novels, not the continuous fabric of a setting, but the disjunction of settings – between the raft on the river and the slave-owning society on the shore in *Huckleberry Finn*, or the Calvinist settlement and the wilderness, the wild forest, in *The Scarlet Letter* – which I see as the explorations of alternative social possibilities. And I mean it and will be prepared to defend it, right now, by quoting authority: as an exploration of alternative social possibilities, the creation, in Marx's phrase, of 'altered circumstances', or, as Brecht, the leading theoretician of the 'epic theatre' or the 'dialectical theatre' and himself immersed in Marxist thought, puts it, 'experiments' to test social truths, to strive 'towards an entirely new social function' (131).

Let me turn now to *Benito Cereno* and mention that since Hollywood has made a film out of the *Amistad* case, I hope, as a spin-off, Melville's story, too, will attract more attention.

Benito Cereno, published in 1855, is based on an actual incident as recorded by a North American sea captain called Amasa Delano, in which slaves under transportation on a Latin American ship mutinied, hijacked the vessel and forced the captain, Benito Cereno, and his navigators (all whites), to change course and take them to Africa. Melville retains the names in his novella.

By the time Melville wrote his story, there had been several slave revolts on land and sea, on land as you know, not just Nat Turner, but Gabriel Prosser, Denmark Vesey[6] and others, and on sea the famous shipboard uprising on the *Amistad* by Spanish slaves who were finally set free by the Supreme Court of the United States.

I would hope that people will turn to *Benito Cereno* because it is one of the most serious examinations of racist ideology in America or anywhere else. The Cold War critics, the American-novel-as-Romance critics, read it, of course, as concerned only incidentally with black slaves and essentially with what Melville himself – in a discussion of Hawthorne – once called 'the power of blackness',[7] which was associated with the Calvinist doctrine of man's innate depravity. Today's critics read it, on the other hand, as concerned with nothing more and nothing less than the institution of slavery. So the essentialist reading is the 'power of blackness', innate depravity, original sin in all of us and the historicist reading is that black spot of American history which created a severe political crisis in the 1850s and plunged the country into civil war five years after Melville wrote *Benito Cereno*.

But essentialist or historicist, it seems to me, what these interpretations overlook is the main point of Melville's tale, the way it is structured, namely, that the uprising has already taken place before the narrative begins, the story has already happened, and what Melville focusses on, instead, is Delano's and Cereno's, particularly Delano's, attempt to make some sense of it, to interpret it within the framework of what Thompson would call their respective 'conceptual systems'.

This means that what the reader of *Benito Cereno* is invited to interpret is not, like Delano and Cereno, the event itself, but *their* interpretations of it. In other words, while Delano and Cereno 'read' the revolt – I am keeping my vocabulary up to date – the reader must read the ideologies of their reading or misreading of it, the ideologies that made slavery not only legal but also seemingly *natural*.

I will not go into the courtroom proceedings that form a sort of appendix to the tale and establish the revolt as a self-evident case for capital punishment on the basis of duly notarized depositions. Nor into the conservative-religious ideology of Benito Cereno, except to recall his famous last words when asked what had caused such a dark shadow to fall on his life – 'The negro' – comparable to Kurtz's 'The horror! The horror!' in Conrad's *The Heart of Darkness* (148), for it is only through some such evocation of the power of blackness that he can understand the revolt as an eruption of man's innate evil.

I would rather focus, as does the novel, on Amasa Delano's ideology which seems the polar opposite of Cereno's, Rousseauistic[8] rather than Calvinist. Unlike the Southern Cereno, he is a Northerner of liberal-secular views untainted by the doctrine of 'malign evil in man' (35). Genial and friendly, he likes the blacks, thinks them lovable and admirable, all of which, however, in no way interferes with his view of slavery as *natural* to, and for, the black race. That the blacks may want liberation from chattel slavery and be prepared to die for it, is to him so unthinkable, so unnatural, that it becomes the source of all those appalling blunders and misunderstandings that constitute the basic continuous narrative substance and interest of the novel.

From the moment he boards the stricken ship as rescuer to the last moment of his departure, he resolutely misinterprets the tableau spread out before him, misreading all the signs, the entire scene, the scenario – a temporary distress caused by adverse gales, a piratical design against his own ship, all kinds of puzzles and suspicions, anything but the possibility of a ship under mutiny by the black slaves.

The surviving whites make what signs and communications they can in order to awaken him to the reality of the situation, but to no effect. For instance, when a white sailor working on a rope-knot suddenly throws the knot to him with the words, 'Undo it, cut it, quick', the narrator comments: 'knot in hand, and knot in head, Captain Delano stood mute' (63).

Delano cannot cut the knot in hand because of the knot in his head, which is the Gordian knot of his ideology. To him, of course, it is no ideology but a simple natural view of the world, of himself, of the black race. But it is, indeed, a knot or a web that ties in a great many things ranging from his perceptions and feelings to the interests of his pocketbook. It is a racist ideology in which there is a perfect fit between the *nature* of the blacks and their position as servants, menials or slaves. And it is the very geniality of Delano that reveals this ideological confusion of the social and the natural.

On the one hand, he perceives blacks as a kind of lovable, faithful animal – he 'took to Negroes, not philanthropically, but genially, as other men to Newfoundland dogs' (71). Elsewhere he sees them as does and fawns (60), even as 'Unsophisticated . . . leopardesses' (61), savage but still noble. The sight of a black infant at his mother's breast causes the exclamation: 'There's naked nature now; pure tenderness and love' (61). On the other hand, it is precisely this 'nature' which, according to Delano, makes the black a natural 'menial' which 'has gained the negro the repute of making the most pleasing body-servant in the world' (40) – even the 'hypochondriacs', Dr. Johnson and Byron, preferring blacks in that role 'almost to the exclusion of the entire white race' (71).

This confusion – and more – is reflected in the name of the intelligent, determined leader of the revolt, Babo – baboon, even Babu? – who, in Delano's presence, plays the role of Cereno's body servant to perfection, in a wonderfully ironic moment holding the razor at his neck under the charade of shaving him. The stratagem works beautifully to the extent that Delano, overcome by 'the beauty of that relationship' (45), the white master/black slave relationship, offers to buy Babo for himself on the spot.

To sum up, *Benito Cereno* is centrally concerned thus, not so much with the institution of slavery as with the exposure of the ideology that accompanies it and the elaborate concealments of that ideology. The truth that is concealed is not recognized by either of the two main characters, nor openly stated by the narrator. This simple truth is that blacks are neither noble nor ferocious animals, and not naturally created by God to be menials and slaves or anything else, that they are just like other human beings of the time and their purpose, like that of other human beings, is liberty. Pleading the case of the *Amistad* mutineers before the Supreme Court, John Quincy Adams,[9] himself a racist, also invoked Nature and God but on the side of liberty, arguing that while the blacks had committed crimes, they were not to be regarded as felons, since their object was to secure liberty which, he declared, was 'the law of Nature and Nature's God on which our fathers placed our own national existence' ('Argument of John Quincy Adams, 1841', Lillian Goldman Law Library, Yale Law School, 9).

As regards the baboon stereotype, an article entitled 'About Niggers', published in the same year in the same magazine that carried Melville's tale, likewise stated that the San Domingo (that is, modern-day Haiti) revolution had clearly demonstrated that the 'nigger' is 'a man, not a baboon' (quoted in Kaplan, 21). This truth, the constructed or the real nature of the black, gets incorporated within the novel, first through the sheer intelligence and steadfastness of purpose in Babo himself; second, through such narrative details as the killing of the owner of the slaves, for, as one of them puts it in his court deposition, 'he and his companions could not otherwise be sure of their liberty' (92); and third, through Melville's small but suggestive departures from the original Amasa Delano's factual account, such as changing the name of the ship from *The Tryal* to *San Dominick*, that is San Domingo, the present-day Haiti, which was the site of the first great slave revolt in the New World.

Huckleberry Finn was published thirty years after *Benito Cereno*, published in the 1880s, although its setting is the slave-owning South-Western society of the 1840s. I do not normally give these details but they are important here, a book of the 1880s placed in the 1840s. It is supposed to be the story of a slave's flight to freedom. But, if this is so, Twain would seem to be flogging a dead horse in political terms by making a plea for abolition of slavery twenty years after Lincoln's Emancipation Act, or Emancipation Proclamation, on January 1, 1863, and, more curiously, in terms of his plot, by narrating the story of freeing a slave who, as we discover at the end, has already been freed.

But actually Twain is flogging no dead horses. Much more than in the case of *Benito Cereno*, his subject is not so much the legal institution of chattel slavery as it is the racist ideology that accompanied and legitimized the legal institution but also – and this is the important point – *survived* it, and was, in fact, extended and intensified. For, following the Civil War and the brief period of so-called 'Radical Reconstruction',[10] racist ideology emerged, North and South, as the nationally accepted legitimizing ideology for the maintenance of white domination and power over the blacks.

And, unlike Melville, Twain confronts this ideology centrally in his novel, inasmuch as he makes his central character, Huck Finn himself, the site of the confrontation, most memorably in that moment of crisis in Chapter 31 when Huck decides to go to hell rather than betray Nigger Jim back into servitude – as history *had* betrayed all the free but still '*Nigger*' Jims of America.

Huckleberry Finn is very much a novel of its time – and ours, too – and that, not only because racist ideologies are healthy and active, in operation, in many places in the world today, but also because Twain is certainly one of those pre-Althusser Althusserians who, in Dollimore's phrase, 'possessed a sophisticated concept of ideology if not the word'.

Consider a Notebook entry[11] ten years after *Huckleberry Finn* was published in which Twain himself described the novel as a book of his in which 'a sound heart and a deformed conscience come into collision and conscience suffers defeat' (619). How close the idea of a *deformed* conscience or consciousness comes to our concept of ideology becomes clear when Twain goes on to say, with pointed irony, obvious irony, 'the conscience – that unerring monitor – can be trained to approve any wild thing you *want* it to approve provided you begin its education early and stick to it' (619). Twain also makes clear the prime function of this socially rather than innately or divinely constructed unerring monitor when he adds that 'the whole community was agreed as to one thing – the awful sacredness of slave property' (619).

How does Twain in *Huckleberry Finn* engineer the defeat of the deformed conscience, the defeat of ideology, or, in our terms, engineer the recognition of ideology and its subversion? Basically, through the conjunction of two primary displacements: one, the radical displacement of the setting from the slave-owning society on the shore along the Mississippi River, to the free-floating raft *on* the river, which presents a situation of 'altered circumstances' or an alternative 'social' experiment in which, as Thompson says, old ideologies may dissolve and a new problematic consciousness emerge to take their place.

Second, the shift in narratorial persona, perspective, voice and language from the official and the genteel to the vernacular. The pseudonym Mark Twain had already offered Samuel Clemens the possibility of distancing himself from genteel culture, even the license to laugh at some of its sacred cows. Out of each of these displacements and, more important, out of their conjunction in the narrative, arise those many ironies, oppositions and conflicts that lead to the defeat of the deformed conscience. But having Huck Finn, the uneducated, uncivilized pariah, tell his own story in his own words marked a far greater, a truly radical, displacement. It pushed the narratorial perspective to the society's economic and social periphery and ultimately thereby brought in the issue of the 'sacredness of slave property' itself.

Out of the many ironies and conflicts generated by this ideological issue, I will focus on what I may call the language conflict, which will include the stereotype as a word loaded with ideological significations – such as the word 'bitch' for a woman, or 'Red' for a communist, and in the present case, 'Nigger' for a slave.

In *Huckleberry Finn*, this conflict operates most fascinatingly not externally or in opposition only; it operates within the vernacular hero himself and within his vernacular language. As to the hero, on the one hand, though not a *verna* or house-born slave, he is still a member of what was the class of so-called 'pore whites' who, after the blacks, constituted the most deprived and depressed class of people under the plantation economy[12] of the Southern states. This left no place for independent farmers who were squeezed out by bigger and bigger estates growing tobacco and cotton. Yet, although belonging to this deprived and depressed class, they were the most rabid of Southern racists, as can be seen from Twain's presentation of Huck's father, Pap.

As to the language, the vernacular is meant to function in the novel as the language of direct, unobtruded, natural perception, unideological perception, and yet it is invaded constantly by the language of culture, especially by its ideologically charged words like Education, Sunday School, Civilization and its binary oppositions such as Sin/Salvation, Black/White and so on. And though Huck himself is always in the end true to his perceptions, to his 'sound heart' in Twain's words, he is nevertheless shown as constantly self-denigrating, constantly awed and swayed by the official language and conceptual systems of his society.

Language conflict is thus an index of the ideological conflict in Huck himself, for we must never forget that, no matter how far his position is from that of the slave-owning gentry, he is a native son of the American South, racist Southern society and inevitably a sharer of its ideology. For, as Twain observes in the Notebook passage about the 'sacredness of slave property', this view was held not only by slave-holders but equally passionately by 'the paupers, the loafers, the tag-rag & bobtail of the whole community' (619).

Which is to say that Huck begins, as does Hester Prynne in *The Scarlet Letter*, from a position of ideological incorporation, and it is his story, his social experience which, like Hester's, leads to his internal conflicts and crises, resulting ultimately in the recognition and repudiation of ideology. Of these crises, or, in Twain's words, the collisions between 'a sound heart and a deformed conscience', I will refer to only two, particularly asking you to note how both are underlined by language conflict and the ironies of the natural and the ideological generated by it.

The first is the famous incident of Huck's practical joke on Jim, the success of which depends on the naïve gullibility of the Nigger or Sambo stereotype. We remember that a similar trick had been routinely played on Jim by Tom Sawyer without any consequences on shore at the beginning of the story, but here leads to a crisis of anger and humiliation on Jim's side and regret on Huck's. For what has intervened between the two incidents is Huck and Jim's common experience on the raft in contradiction to the governing codes and social practices on shore. So that when Huck decides finally to apologize, this is how he puts it: 'It took me fifteen minutes before I could work myself up and humble myself to a nigger – but I done it, and I warn't sorry for it afterwards, neither' (Ch. 15, 105).

Despite the word 'nigger', or perhaps because of it, this is one of the great counter-demonstrations produced by the experiment in altered social conditions represented by the raft. For what we see here is the black man emerging from the ideologically imposed constructed stereotype into ordinary humanness, vulnerable to anger, hurt pride, grief, as much as to the claims of friendship, affection and solidarity. And Huck, in recognizing Jim's humanity, endorses his own, so that the racial stereotyping stands negated on both sides.

But the more decisive break with ideology occurs in Chapter 31, where Huck has to choose between continuing his abetment of Jim's escape and giving the whereabouts of the runaway slave to the lawful owner, thereby approving himself by becoming an upright citizen. At this point we have the 'deformed conscience' and the 'sound heart' again, the 'deformed conscience', our ideology, mounting its entire attack this time with the ultimate weapon of religious rhetoric. In preacherish language it shows him up for what he is: wicked, depraved, sinful, rightly slapped in the face by Providence, until Huck finally kneels down to pray, and then writes the letter to Jim's owner, and, all at once, as he says, feels 'all washed clean of sin' (Ch. 31, 269).

In the end, of course, it is the 'sound heart' that wins and the 'deformed conscience' or ideology that suffers defeat, and Huck tears up the letter in full knowledge that this decisive act would mean the abandonment of salvation itself:

> It was a close place . . . I was a trembling, because I'd got to decide, forever, betwixt two things, and I know'd it. I studied a minute, sort of holding my breath, and then says to myself: 'All right, then, I'll go to hell'.
>
> (Ch. 31, 270–1)

The saving moment, and this is what I meant by language conflict, finds expression in and through the language of domination, showing the penetration that ideology's conceptual systems can attain in ourselves.

Turning to *The Scarlet Letter*, I will make a few quick points on precisely this question of Hester's internal struggle vis-à-vis ideology and then focus entirely on the process of ideological subversion in it through social experience. First of all, to rehearse the fact, it is the story of a woman, Hester Prynne, who has committed adultery and is punished for it. The story is set in the 17th-century theocracy of Massachusetts, where 'religion and law were almost identical' (Ch. 2, 113), so that one can say of it what Engels says of the Middle Ages in *Ludwig Feuerbach and the Outcome of Classical German Philosophy*, that it 'knew no other form of ideology than religion and theology' (35). This, then, is the ideological situation.

Two, if Twain's basic strategy for subversion is linguistic, Hawthorne's is symbolist. The novel is dominated by a single sign, the Letter A, which emblematizes Hester's adultery, which itself, to the Puritan mind, is a *type* of sin, the ante-type or transcendental signified of which is the original sin – A for Adam, 'in Adam's fall / We sinned all'.[13] Hawthorne's symbolism challenges the typological[14] or allegorical one-to-one interpretation by introducing a plurality of meanings, thus subverting the single ideological interpretation of Hester's deed by viewing it from a plurality of perspectives, including the social, the political and the historical.

Hawthorne thus displays what C. Wright Mills once called the sociological imagination, 'the capacity to range from the most impersonal and remote transformations to the most intimate features of the human self – and to see the relations between the two' (7). Indeed, in Chapter 13, on which I shall shortly focus, Hawthorne associates the ideological revolution in Hester's consciousness specifically with the European revolutions of the time, when 'Men of the sword had overthrown nobles and kings', and 'Men bolder than these had overthrown and rearranged . . . the whole system of ancient prejudice, wherewith was linked much of ancient principle' (Ch. 13, 181). Not the word, but 'deformed conscience', 'prejudice', 'principle' – these are some of the approximations of what today we call 'ideology'.

Third, and most important, the process of experience in Hawthorne is far more sophisticated than in a writer like Twain – both of them fit into the same thesis, but I must make a distinction between them. Hawthorne is more sophisticated both novelistically and sociologically, recalling James and Thompson rather than Twain, in his marvellous understanding and depiction of what 'experience' means as a junction of consciousness and being and how it can be generated not only by historical transformation but by other kinds of happenings – crises of subsistence, unemployment, imprisonment – all of which are particularly apropos to this text, as is Thompson's further observation that in the face of such crises, old conceptual systems crumble yielding place to new problematics.

It is only in this sense that, while focussing on Hester's experience, for instance, Hawthorne can also say that her lover, the clergyman Dimmesdale, has had *no* experience. If we think of the nature of the sin/crime, it is the only crime that cannot be committed individually! So, what did Hawthorne mean by saying that Hester has had experience but Dimmesdale none? I shall clarify shortly, but here let me only say that *The Scarlet Letter* is a novel of experience in this sense rather than a narrative of events. It is barren of events and is concerned not so much with what has happened to Hester as it is with her apprehension and her measure in her consciousness of what has happened to her as a social being.

As a social being, Hester's story, like Huck's, begins in and from a position of ideology. Until her passionate love affair and her sexual awakening, she is in all conscience a member of good standing of the Church and the Colony. And if her story ends with something approaching repudiation of ideology, this happens after seven difficult years of ideological self-division, years during which she lives what Kate Chopin in *The Awakening* – another great late 19th-century novel about a woman – calls 'the dual life, that outward existence which conforms, the inward life which questions' (Ch. 7, 35).

In other words, if the questioning or ideological self-conflict is resolved in Chapter 13, it is after a long and painful interplay between her consciousness and the crises of her social being, not just the thwarting of her passion, but her imprisonment, the public trial, the emblematization, stigmatization, followed by public ostracism and, above all, the crisis of subsistence, all of which drives her to the farthest edge of the settlement for abode and to needlework for a living, the loss of caste as well as class. (By the way, in the early 19th century on both sides of the Atlantic, a quick shorthand for describing the working class was seamstresses, workers in sweatshops, so in her becoming a needlewoman, though Hawthorne makes it an art and a craft, she does lose both caste and class.)

And more constantly, the difficulties of a single mother, something we would understand better today, of a working mother of a daughter who, dressed in scarlet clothes, is herself perceived as a replication and reminder of the sinful letter. Indeed, her questioning in Chapter 13 which is called 'Another View of Hester' – Hawthorne could as easily have called it 'A View of Another Hester' – begins precisely with her domestic situation and then reaches out to the social and the historical situation. By now, as the narrator tells us, her life has turned 'from passion and feeling to thought' (Ch. 13, 181) and the scarlet letter A itself, the badge she wears, has become to her an indication not of sin but her 'position in respect to society' (Ch. 13, 180).

First, her daughter growing up 'amid a host of difficulties. Everything was against her. The world was hostile' (Ch. 13, 182). But then, as the narrator goes on, 'the same dark question often arose into her mind, with reference to the whole race of womanhood. Was existence worth accepting to the happiest among them?' (Ch. 13, 182). And, finally, from the personal problem and the gender question, to the entire social structure: 'As a first step, the whole system of society is to be torn down, and built anew' (Ch. 13, 182). This was what I suggested earlier, ideology as a device, or ideological exploration connecting the innermost subjective with the largest questions of social structure itself.

But what about Dimmesdale – a question I asked earlier – the secret sharer of Hester's love and guilt? Why, though a sensitive and tortured man throughout, does he not arrive ever, not for a minute in his life, at any similar questions and thoughts? Hawthorne is a thinker, and the clearest answer is given by the novelist himself:

> For years . . . Hester had looked from this estranged point of view at human institutions, and whatever priests and legislators had established. . . . The minister, on the other hand, had never gone through an experience calculated to lead him beyond the scope of generally received laws. . . . At the head of the social system, as the clergyman of that day stood, he was only the more trammelled by its regulations, its principles, and even its prejudices.
>
> (Ch. 18, 202–3)

Starting from the same ideological position (or with the same prejudice), Hester's experience has led to the subversion, or whatever you wish to call it, and Dimmesdale's lack of it to the confirmation, of ideology, something that benefits and is maintained by the ruling class.

I would like to sum up by saying that not all literature is equally vulnerable to ideology, that, on the contrary, the novels I have discussed today seem to foreground precisely this vulnerability to ideology as one of their central explorations. And I would like to ask, in conclusion, what possible benefit can accrue, to whom and for what purpose, by subjecting such classics to procedures of symptomatic ideological critique.

I would rather reverse the order, as I have done in this lecture, and read these classics themselves as novelistic critiques of ideology. As Belinsky[15] once said, 'pure, abstract . . . art never existed anywhere' (455), 'Art is the *immediate* contemplation of truth' (180), ' Art is the representation of reality, the reduplicated or, as it were, newly created world' (452). And what, after all, in the field of human and social phenomena, is so preposterous in recognizing that the same truths may be accessible to literary representation as to abstract thought?

And if there are 'scientific' theorists today who deny such cognitive power to literature, we must not forget those earlier 'scientists' who saw in literature an anticipation or confirmation of their theories and concepts. We have Freud's famous acknowledgement of indebtedness to no scientific predecessors but only a few artists like Sophocles and Shakespeare.[16] (Incidentally, those of you who have read Harold Bloom's *The Western Canon* will recall how far he takes this: in his chapter on Freud he states that 'Freud is essentially prosified Shakespeare' (345), and instead of a Freudian reading of *Hamlet* he has a Shakespearean reading of Freud!) We have Marx's comment that 'Shakespeare paints a brilliant picture of the nature of *money*' (*Early Writings*, 377), Engels's declaration that he had learnt more about 1816 to 1848 French society, even in its economic details, from Balzac 'than from all the professed historians, economists and statisticians of the period together'(*Marx and Engels on Literature*, 115).

Basically, in the field of the human and the social, this is a false quarrel. Thus, instead of seeing literary classics as ideological productions to be unmasked by science or theory, I would see them in Brecht's terms when he talks of a theatre for a 'scientific age' which demonstrates a 'knowledge of . . . human relations, of human behaviour' (26) and 'encourages those thoughts and feelings' which help transformation and improvement (190). For, in Althusser's words, Brecht's 'principal aim is to produce a critique of the spontaneous ideology in which men live' (*For Marx*, 144). So science or literature, my submission is that the cognition, not necessarily the word, can be as accessible not to all kinds of novels but certainly to a particular kind of novel.

Thank you very much. It has been a real pleasure and an honour to deliver these lectures.

Notes

1 Adam Schaff (1913–2006), Polish Marxist philosopher of Jewish origin, studied economics in Paris and philosophy in Poland and Moscow, returned to Warsaw University and was considered the official ideologue of the Polish United Workers Party.

2 Destutt de Tracy (1784–1836), French Enlightenment aristocrat and philosopher, who coined the term 'Ideology'.

3 Max Weber (1864–1920), German sociologist, philosopher, jurist and political economist, who is cited with Durkheim and Marx as among the founders of sociology. He is best known for his thesis combining economic sociology and the sociology of religion set forth in his book *The Protestant Ethic and the Spirit of Capitalism.*

4 Parsonian Functionalism is named after Talcott Parsons (1902–79), an American sociologist, whose work focusses attention on the power of the social system to influence the social behaviour of individuals. Functionalism addresses society as a whole in terms of its constituent elements – norms, customs, traditions and institutions.

5 Louis Althusser (1918–90), French Marxist philosopher, born in Algeria, educated at the Pierre École Normale Superieure in Paris where he became Professor of Philosophy. A long-time member of the French Communist Party, he argued against the threats that he saw attacking the theoretical foundations of Marxism. His life was marked by intense periods of insanity which led to his killing his wife and being committed for three years to a psychiatric hospital.

6 Nat Turner (1800–31), enslaved African American preacher, led a four-day rebellion in Virginia of both enslaved and free black people which caused the death of 60 white people. Troops were called in, an estimated 120 black people were killed, Turner was hunted and found, tried, convicted and hanged.

  Gabriel Prosser (1776–1800), a literate, enslaved blacksmith, planned a slave rebellion in the Richmond area in the summer of 1800, information about it was leaked and Prosser and twenty-five others were captured and executed.

  Denmark Vesey (1767–1822), a literate, skilled carpenter and leader of African Americans in Charleston, South Carolina, was accused of planning a slave uprising, convicted and executed.

7 'The power of blackness' was a phrase used by Melville in an essay on Hawthorne, 'Hawthorne and his Mosses', which appeared in two instalments (August 17 and August 24, 1850) in *The Literary World*, edited and published by his friend, Evert Duyckinck. Melville speaks of the other side of Hawthorne, his 'great power of blackness', which derives its force from the Calvinistic sense of Innate Depravity and Original Sin.

  John Calvin (1509–64), French theologian, pastor and reformer in Geneva during the Protestant revolution. Calvinism emphasizes the doctrine of predestination and the sovereignty of God in the salvation of the human soul from death and eternal damnation.

8 Jean-Jacques Rousseau (1712–78), Genevan philosopher, writer and composer, whose *Discourse on Inequality* and *Social Contract* are cornerstones of modern political and social thought and influenced the Enlightenment throughout Europe as well as the French Revolution.

9 African slaves being shipped to Cuba on the Spanish schooner *La Amistad* in 1839 broke their shackles, killed the captain and cook, took over the vessel and demanded a return to Africa. They were tricked by the navigators and the ship was apprehended near Long Island, New York, by the United States Coast Guard and taken into custody. The case was heard by the United States Supreme Court in 1841 where the mutineers were represented by John Quincy Adams, former president of the United States, who won the case, and thirty-five of them were returned to Africa.

  John Quincy Adams (1767–1848), sixth president of the United States from 1825 to 1829, formerly Secretary of State, and later a member of the United States Senate and the United States House of Representatives from Massachusetts, was the eldest son of John Adams, second president of the United States.

10 'Radical Reconstruction' was the period of American history from 1863 to 1867 following the Civil War. From 1863 Congress directed the eleven former Confederate states to end secession and slavery, granting citizenship and civil rights

to former slaves. But with Lincoln's assassination, Andrew Johnson, a Democrat from Tennessee and a former slaveholder, became president and allowed Southern states to determine the rights of former slaves. Radical Republicans fought back, but while they reasserted those rights, their policies also gave rise to white supremacist groups and the Ku Klux Klan.

11 Mark Twain prepared several selections from *Huckleberry Finn* for his 1895–6 world lecture tour and had a long list of passages he used. As he neared Australia, however, he realized that his schedule there required as many as five performances in some of the larger cities and he had to plan different programmes to avoid repetition. He considered selections from Chapter 8 and Chapter 15 and wrote an Introduction in Notebook #35 from which the sentences in the lecture are quoted.

12 Plantation economy is an economy relying on cash crops like sugar cane, cotton and tobacco as a source of income. In the United States, plantations were concentrated in the South and used slave labour.

13 See Ch. 1, Note 1.

14 'Typology' is the study of types, the classification of languages, artefacts and the model of personality types. See the discussion of the Oblomov type and Dobrolyubov in Ch. 2, Note 12.

15 See Ch. 2, Note 12.

16 Sigmund Freud (1856–1939), the father of psychoanalysis, was inspired by Sophocles and Shakespeare. In *The Interpretation of Dreams* he discusses several of Shakespeare's plays, among them *Hamlet, Julius Caesar, Timon of Athens, A Midsummer Night's Dream* and, of course, Sophocles's *Oedipus*, which lends its name to his famous 'Oedipus Complex'. He also records his admiration for a large number of literary figures: 'the eternal Homer, the gigantic Dante, the incomparable Shakespeare, the glorious Goethe' (474).

Works cited

Adams, John Quincy. *Argument of John Quincy Adams, Before the Supreme Court of the United States: In the Case of the United States, Appellants vs. Cinque, and Others, Africans, Captured in the Schooner Amistad, by Lieut. Gedney. Delivered on the 24th of February and 1st of March, 1841.* Lillian Goldman Law Library, Yale Law School, pp. 1–136.

Althusser, Louis. *For Marx.* Tr. Ben Brewster. London: Penguin Books, 1969.

———. *Lenin and Philosophy and Other Essays.* Tr. Ben Brewster. New York: Monthly Review Press, 1971.

Belinsky, Vissarion. *Selected Philosophical Works.* Moscow: Foreign Languages Publishing House, 1956.

Bercovitch, Sacvan. *Ideology and Classic American Literature.* Cambridge: Cambridge University Press, 1986.

Bloom, Harold. *The Western Canon: The Books and Schools of the Ages.* New York: Riverhead Books, 1995, pp. 345–66.

Brecht, Bertolt. *Brecht on Theatre.* Ed. and Tr. John Willett. New York: Hill and Wang, 1964.

Chopin, Kate. *The Awakening.* Introduction by Kenneth Eble. New York: Capricorn Books, 1964.

Conrad, Joseph. *The Heart of Darkness*. Ed. D.C.R.A. Goonetilleke. Peterborough, ON: Broadview Press, 2003.

Dollimore, Jonathan. *Radical Tragedy: Religion, Ideology and Power in the Drama of Shakespeare and his Contemporaries*. Durham: Duke University Press, 2004.

Engels, Friedrich. *Ludwig Feuerbach and the Outcome of Classical German Philosophy*. Ed. C.P. Dutt. New York: International Publishers, 1941.

Freud, Sigmund. *The Interpretation of Dreams*. Tr. James Strachey. New York: Basic Books Publishers, 1955.

Giddons, Anthony. *Central Problems in Social Theory*. London: Macmillan, 1979.

Gramsci, Antonio. *Selections from the Prison Notebooks of Antonio Gramsci*. Ed. and Tr. Quintin Hoare and Geoffrey Nowell Smith. New York: International Publishers, 1951.

Habermas, Jurgen. 'Technology and Science as Ideology'. *Toward a Rational Society*. Tr. Jeremy J. Shapiro. Boston: Beacon Press, 1970.

Hawthorne, Nathaniel. 'Dedicatory Letter'. *"The Snow Image" and other Twice-Told Tales. Writings of Nathaniel Hawthorne*. Boston and New York: Houghton Mifflin Company, 1900, Vol. 3.

———. *The Scarlet Letter. The Complete Novels and Selected Tales of Nathaniel Hawthorne*. Ed. with an Introduction by Norman Holmes Pearson. New York: The Modern Library, 1937.

James, Henry. *The Princess Casamassima*. 2 Vols. London: Macmillan, 1921.

Jehlen, Myra. 'The Novel and the Middle Class in America'. *Ideology and Classic American Literature*. Cambridge: Cambridge University Press, 1986, pp. 125–44.

Kaplan, Justice. 'Herman Melville and the American National Sin: The Meaning of *Benito Cereno*'. *Journal of Negro History*, 2 parts, 41 (1956), 311–38; 42 (1957), 11–37.

Kaul, A. N. *History, Sociology and the American Romance*. Shimla: Indian Institute of Advanced Study, 1990.

Macherey, Pierre. *A Theory of Literary Production*. Tr. Geoffrey Wall. London: Routledge & Kegan Paul, 1978.

Marx, Karl. *A Contribution to the Critique of Political Economy*. Tr. N.I. Stoke. Calcutta: Bharati Library, 1904.

———. 'Economic and Philosophical Manuscripts'. *Early Writings*. Ed. Quintin Hoare. Introduced by Lucio Colletti. New York: Vintage Books, 1975, pp. 279–400.

Marx, Karl and Friedrich Engels. *The German Ideology: Parts I & III*. London: Lawrence Wishart, 1940.

———. *Marx and Engels on Literature & Art: A Selection of Writings*. Ed. Lee Barandall and Stefan Morawski. Introduction by Stefan Morawski. St. Louis, Milwaukee: Telos Press, 1973.

Melville, Herman. 'Hawthorne and His Mosses'. *The Literary World*, August 17 and August 24 1850. Also in *Herman Melville*, ed. Harison Hayford, New York: The Library of New York, 1984, 1154–71, p. 1159.

———. *Benito Cereno. Melville's Short Novels*. Ed. Dan McCall. New York and London: W.W. Norton & Co., 2002, pp. 34–102.

Mills, C. Wright. *The Sociological Imagination*. Oxford and New York: Oxford University Press, 1959, rpt. 2000.

Thompson, E.P. *The Poverty of Theory and Other Essays*. London: The Merlin Press, 1978.

Twain, Mark. *The Adventures of Huckleberry Finn: The Works of Mark Twain*. Ed. Victor Fischer and Lin Salamo. With the late Walter Blair. Berkeley, Los Angeles, London: University of California Press, 2003, Vol. 8.

———. Appendix F, 'Mark Twain's Revisions for Public Reading, 1895–6'. *The Works of Mark Twain*. Ed. Victor Fischer and Lin Salamo. With the late Walter Blair. Berkeley, Los Angeles, London: University of California Press, 2003, Vol. 8, pp. 617–21.

Wordsworth, William. *Preface to the Lyrical Ballads, 1802. The Norton Anthology of English Literature*, 2 Vols. New York and London: W.W. Norton & Co., 1979. Vol. 2, pp. 1959–75.

4 'What is past, or passing, or to come'

Hawthorne and the idea of historical continuity

In my lecture today, I am going to take a very narrow aspect of Hawthorne, and I would like to make it clear at the outset that it is not my contention that this is the only way of looking at Hawthorne. The aspect I am going to explore today is indicated by my somewhat fancy title and is an aspect that I do not see examined as much in modern criticism of him as I would personally like. Or at least not quite in the way in which I would personally feel satisfied that a fellow scholar has said things with clarity and I need not grope and struggle. Matters were slightly different when Henry James wrote his book on Hawthorne because he singled out for special emphasis two aspects of his subject: one, of course, the deeper psychology, and the second, what James called Hawthorne's 'historic consciousness' (67), though I must add that James thought that in Hawthorne the historic consciousness operated without 'the apparatus of a historian' (4).

T.S. Eliot, writing on the Hawthorne-James relationship several years later, again singled out these two aspects, and whereas he seems to have given the palm to Henry James in the matter of psychology, Eliot allows that Hawthorne is somewhat superior to Henry James in the matter of historical consciousness. 'In one thing alone', Eliot wrote in 1918, 'Hawthorne is more solid than James: he had a very acute historical sense. . . . Both men had that sense of the past which is peculiarly American, but in Hawthorne this sense exercised itself in a grip on the past itself; in James it is a sense of the sense' (quoted in Kaul, *Hawthorne*, Introduction, 4). Well-known words but, taken as a whole, they have caused me problems. I would myself not think of using the phrase 'more solid' for Hawthorne who would himself be horrified if he thought of his work as more solid than anyone else's work. Slightly more puzzling, or at least obfuscating, is Eliot's phrase 'a sense of the sense'; I half understand and half do not understand what he means when he says that James had merely 'a sense of the sense', but what can be misleading I think sometimes is his phrase 'sense of the past'.

It will be my attempt today to suggest that to the historical imagination any sharp distinctions between the past and the present and the future do not seem valid. The whole point of the exercise of the historical imagination as we have come to understand it in modern times is to erase to the extent possible these distinctions – the finished quality of the past, the finished quality of the historical event. It would be more something like the concept of a historical continuum or continuity. But supposing for the time being I was to argue and say, why not a sense of the future? Which is equally characteristic of Hawthorne and, I might say, as peculiarly American as Eliot would say that a sense of the past is, and I would suggest that this sense of the future enters into what I consider the first exercise in expression, if not art, in America, Bradford's *Plymouth Colony*.[1] The way I read that book, it looks forward towards the future more than to Europe, but particularly in the first chapter where, as you will recall, Bradford is setting out itemized reasons for the removal of this small band of Puritans to America, and as his final reason he says: 'Lastly, (and which was not the least) a great hope and inward zeal they had of laying some good foundation' (Bk. I, Ch. 4, 25).

This idea of laying foundations connects basically, I think, the present with the future, and is, in my opinion, as characteristic of Hawthorne as a sense of the past, and I am going to quote a few places from some of Hawthorne's works to make this clear, beginning with the two 'John Endicott' stories. Let me cite the closing words of 'Endicott and the Red Cross':

> We look back through the mist of ages, and recognize, in the rending of the Red Cross from New England's banner, the first omen of that deliverance which our forefathers consummated after the bones of the stern Puritan had lain more than a century in the dust.

> (1018)

If your point of reference is the time of the writing of the story, it is a reference to the past. If you take the time of the story as the present time, then it is certainly a reference towards the future. Likewise, in 'The Maypole of Merry Mount', you may remember that John Endicott with his sword, with one stroke of his sword, fells the Maypole and Hawthorne concludes:

> And Endicott, the severest Puritan of all who laid the rock foundation of New England, lifted the wreath of roses from the ruin of the Maypole, and threw it, with his own gauntleted hand, over the heads of the Lord and Lady of May. It was a deed of prophecy.

> (889)

The same comment that I made about 'Endicott and the Red Cross' applies here – in one sense it is a reference to the past, but in another sense to the future. And if you turn to *The Scarlet Letter*, Chapter 1, the well-known words, 'The founders of a new colony, whatever Utopia of human virtue and happiness they might originally project' (112), indicate an ironic reference backwards to precisely the kind of holy commonwealth or the Bradford cooperative experiment in land farming that is given in *Plymouth Colony*. So here is an ironic reference right at the beginning of the book to the past. But the closing words in the last chapter express the 'firm belief' of Hawthorne's 'destined prophetess', or prophetess manqué if you would like to put it that way,

> that, at some brighter period, when the world should have grown ripe for it, in Heaven's own time, a new truth would be revealed, in order to establish the whole relation between man and woman on a surer ground of mutual happiness.
>
> (240)

The House of the Seven Gables has a contemporary setting and is supposed to be Hawthorne's novel about his own time, and yet, as you will remember, through the house itself and through the histories of the two families, the Pyncheons and the Maules, we have a going back to the 17th century but not merely that, via Holgrave for instance, we have again a reference to the future:

> As to the main point, – may we never live to doubt it! – as to the better centuries that are coming, the artist [Holgrave] was surely right. His error lay in supposing that this age, more than any past or future one, is destined to see the tattered garments of Antiquity exchanged for a new suit.
>
> (Ch. 12, 351)

So past, present, and future are once again in play in such references. And finally, briefly, from *The Blithedale Romance*, where Coverdale says of the Blithedale experiment in the very last chapter words that I will repeat later: 'More and more, I feel that we had struck upon what ought to be a truth. Posterity may dig it up, and profit by it' (584). Which gives to an experiment somewhat futuristic in itself, a further or farther futuristic reference.

Before proceeding to a slightly more detailed examination of the novels, I would like to add to the James/Eliot theses of Hawthorne's historic consciousness, the following original theses:

1   That while the three novels may deal with past, present or future separately, what we see more often is what has been called transtemporality or the idea of historical continuity.

2   That in this, Hawthorne is different from some other American writers to whom place was more important than time, America more important than the connection with Europe.

3   That what protects Hawthorne's work from the more naïve expressions of futuristic, millennial, utopian thinking is an irony, one among many he uses. I think he uses narrative irony, he uses modern irony, but this one I can only call historical irony, by which I mean a constant juxtaposition: on the one hand, Hawthorne's sure grasp of the historical realities of time and place, and on the other, his engagement with whatever utopias of human virtue and happiness, whatever good foundations, whatever schemes in the goodness of their heart men might conceive for the betterment of humanity. And last qualification, that he examines the millennial possibilities sometimes with sympathy, sometimes with doubt, but almost always in the light of reality.

With this introduction, I would like to turn now to the three American novels, *The Scarlet Letter*, *The House of the Seven Gables* and *The Blithedale Romance*, published within a short span of two years (1850–2) in rapid succession. *American* novels, not because they were written by an American, but because it seems to me that the matter, the matter of America, is in some very profound way the subject of these novels. Indeed, if they were all written in a uniform fictional mode and if Hawthorne were a little more Trollope-ian – he wanted to be a Trollope, he wanted to be solid – if he were a little more Trollope-ian, one might easily take these three novels, put them in the same covers, and entitle them *America: A Historical Trilogy*. But, of course, the modes differ and something more which I would like to put to you. It is very tempting, particularly in the light of my fancy quotation from William Butler Yeats's 'Sailing to Byzantium', to classify the novels thus: *The Scarlet Letter* – past; *The House of the Seven Gables* – what is passing or present and *The Blithedale Romance* – what is to come. I think this gives some sense of Hawthorne's idea, the way he apprehended history as a kind of continuity, but it also tends to suppress or ignore the cross-references within each work. To make of *The Scarlet Letter* merely an examination of the past, the finished-ness of the past, would just not bear scrutiny, so that I think what I will have to do, it might take a little longer, is to examine these three novels separately.

The Scarlet Letter as a beginning statement: Hawthorne's examination of the foundations of New England, by extension America, and by further extension the entire modern period of Western history which turns out to have been co-terminus or co-extensive with the history of America from the 17th to the 19th centuries, not just America in its essential interest but perhaps equally Europe. I shall do this examination by a slightly detailed analysis of just one chapter – the book is too well-known for me to spend time discussing other things generally, so I would rather examine one spot in it with some care. And this chapter happens to be one that is called 'Another View of Hester', one of the two that Hawthorne devotes to an examination of whatever is going on within Hester's mind. It is a review chapter, it could, in different hands, become an internal monologue; it could be one of those experience chapters where what has happened to Hester is being examined, is becoming a part of her worldview, of her morality, of her spirituality and so on. 'Another', because he has already given us one such, 'Hester at Her Needle', but I think 'Another' in a slightly more important sense: not the world's view of Hester but this time, rather, Hester's view of her world. Or, to put it slightly differently: what has happened to Hester during these seven years which has led to this radical, profound change in a woman who must originally have been of the same persuasion as the other Calvinists who would take the time and trouble to leave Europe and come to America?

Now, it is in this chapter that I think resides most pointedly Hawthorne's reading of the historical meaning of her individual experience, and I would like to start by saying that in this reading, once again, there is a connection drawn between Hester and history, a little overtly. First of all, of course, this is one of the two or three places where Hester is overtly connected with an actual historical personage, namely, Anne Hutchinson. Had Pearl not 'come to her', we are told in this chapter, 'she might have come down to us in history hand in hand with Anne Hutchinson, as the foundress of a religious sect. She might, in one of her phases, have been a prophetess' (Ch. 13, 181–2). But, more interestingly, unlike many other writers of America at that time, Hester's speculations move from the personal and the familial to the feminist and the social, and there is a wider reference to a continuity with what was going on in Europe.

> It was an age [says Hawthorne] in which the human intellect, newly emancipated, had taken a more active and wider range than for many centuries before. Men of the sword had overthrown nobles and kings. Men bolder than these had overthrown and rearranged – not actually but within the sphere of theory, which was their most real abode – the whole system of ancient prejudice, wherewith was linked much of ancient principle. Hester Prynne imbibed this spirit. She assumed a freedom of speculation, then common enough on the other side of the Atlantic, but which our forefathers, had they known it, would have held to be a deadlier crime than that stigmatized by the scarlet letter.
>
> (Ch. 13, 181)

Now this is an overt but in my opinion an unnecessary historical reference, because as a novelist of the historical imagination, it is not required that

Hawthorne show this 'historical spirit' hovering above human beings living their actual lives, the day-to-day concerns of love and family, passions, contradictions, confusions. It is the hallmark of the historical imagination to show the historical spirit working in and through what might otherwise be called the mere existential problems of particular characters, including the profound confusions into which they fall, the contradictions they experience and so on. Thus, if you read the chapter carefully, Hawthorne does not begin with this formulation. It is not as though he is suggesting that Hester Prynne had read the latest books transported across the Atlantic. Not at all. The process he is suggesting is somewhat as follows: Hester is reviewing the ruin of her own life. Would she ever again be happy? The answer is no. Would the daughter, Pearl, ever be happy? No. What about women in general? Is their lot any better? The answer is no. And it is only then that she goes on to question the world in ways larger than the merely feminist and at one point, of course, comes close to making a kind of statement when she says: 'As a first step', and I repeat, 'As a first step, the whole system of society is to be torn down, and built up anew' (Ch. 13, 182). But she does not begin with the whole system of society being torn down. She has not read the trans-Atlantic thinkers. She is concerned with her own problems, herself, her daughter, family, women in general, society in general.

I can merely indicate but not give a full account – which can only come from reading with care – of this great characteristic of Hawthorne's art, this marvellous combination of the personal and the historical, this apprehension of what to him might come as the historical spirit now through, and I am using his own phrase in 'The Custom House', the 'modes of passion' (103), the modes of passion of people who lived then. And when one comes across this kind of art, one wonders, what is the relevance of invoking the name of a romancer? How does that explain, how does that help romance, allegory, are there not these key spots in Hawthorne which make them not trivial phrases to use but actually reductive and irrelevant? I would myself, if I had to use a phrase other than my own, use what Wright Mills calls the 'sociological imagination', which he defines – a definition that has been cited in the chapter on Ideology – as

> the capacity to range from the most impersonal and remote transformations to the most intimate features of the human self – and to see the relations between the two. Back of its use there is always the urge to know the social and historical meaning of the individual in the society and in the period in which he has his quality and his being.
>
> (7)

Words which I think fit like a glove some of these effects in Hawthorne.

If at this point I theorize, generalize and ask, what is Hawthorne's judgement, verdict, what is the final result of his examination of the beginnings, the fountainhead, of either American civilization or modernity in Europe, I think something like the following might be a plausible answer: certainly not an organic state harmoniously combining the intimate, the inner, the personal, with the religious, the political, the social, not certainly this dream of a holy commonwealth. This was to pass. What the 17th century was about was rather the image that Hawthorne constantly uses with regard to the Puritans – the image of iron. It was about the release of a new force and a new energy and a serious purpose of building the material world, which new spirit can put to flight, as in 'The Maypole of Merry Mount', the older, luxurious feudal world, without even exerting the arm. It is ready to die, and a new energy will take over.

At the same time, a world where, if there is any harmony to be expected, it is not going to be the harmony of a total state, be it theocratic or any other, it is a world of personal liberty, not a utopia of virtue and happiness but closer to life, liberty and the *pursuit* of happiness, rather than virtue and happiness. Whereas this is the positive possibility of this world – individual freedom, personal relations, the domestic world – I think Hawthorne also suggests some of the negative possibilities, among them the isolation, the heavier psychological burden such as Hester has to bear, Dimmesdale has to bear, and perhaps even an inner fragmentation. I sometimes like to read the characters of Dimmesdale, Hester and Chillingworth allegorically and make them stand for the head, the heart and the body, passion, thought, spirit, and remember Yeats's celebration of the wholeness of being in 'Among School Children' where 'The body is not bruised to pleasure soul, / Nor beauty born out of its own despair, / Nor blear-eyed wisdom out of midnight oil' (Stanza VIII). It is as though the lines were written for these three characters: the bruising of Dimmesdale of his body, the beauty born out of its own despair, so that on the negative side we see the beginnings possibly of what Emerson[2] would later call the fragmentation of man: 'The state of society is one in which the members have suffered amputation from the trunk, and strut about so many walking monsters . . . but never a man' ('The American Scholar', 25–6). And without going into details I think this comes across if we see *The Scarlet Letter* not merely as a story about the Puritans, but if we see it, number one, as Hester's tragedy played against the grain of the world that the Puritans wished established; number two, if we try to examine the meaning of Hester's tragic challenge; number three, if we try to examine the meaning of Hester's tragic illumination which makes her rise above her world at one point and judge it, judge it not in its own terms but in larger terms, perspectives maybe of the future as I suggested – 'As a first step, the whole system of society is to be torn down, and built up anew'.

If put in discursive prose, I think this is what Hawthorne would be saying in *The Scarlet Letter*.

In *The House of the Seven Gables*, the sense of historical continuity, of seeing the past coming into the present and so on, is not in my opinion as subtly done as it is in *The Scarlet Letter*. Indeed, I think *The House of the Seven Gables* is a very obvious kind of book, and it is amazing that up until Matthiessen's time (not to mention Yvor Winters and Henry James) it was regarded as Hawthorne's best. People see it as Hawthorne's one sustained realistic novel. I do think it has realism, but I am sorry I can only call it the realism of trivial presentation. It is a trivial kind of realism; it goes only into how things are done, not what things are. In its essential interest it is in fact less psychological and perhaps more allegorical than *The Scarlet Letter* or even *The Blithedale Romance*. It deals more nakedly with ideas and with personifications. And on the subject of historical continuity, I do not have to dwell on it; the personifications are primarily the house itself and of course, the continuous history of the two families, the Pyncheons and the Maules, the patricians on the one hand and the artisans, the plebeians on the other.

With regard to the house, I sometimes look at this novel and compare it with *Howard's End* and ask myself, to what extent is this a place and to what extent is it a repository of time? I could use here a term from Bakhtin,[3] the early Russian structuralist who influenced some of the later ones a great deal. The term is 'chronotope', a place that is chronos, that is time, that is history, as well as space, and I think this word gives us the sense of the house which was built on an expropriated piece of land and where the original wrong has been perpetrated, generation after generation.

With regard to the question of original wrong, I take this once again as an example of Hawthornian transformation, an example of how Hawthorne uses theological concepts, theological concepts and images, to think not theologically but socially and historically. Original sin, original wrong. The original wrong in *The House of the Seven Gables* is, as you know, of an economic nature. It is dispossession. Cooper talked a great deal about the original sin of American civilization, but to Cooper, with his kind of thinking, the original wrong was the dispossession of the Red Man. It was based on race. Hawthorne, much more discerning, makes it, from the beginning, looking forward to his own time, looking forward to levelling democracy, makes it realistically enough a question not between the vanishing Red Man and the White Man, he makes it a point from the beginning about the lower orders and the higher orders. I do not know how to give them class labels in the American situation: the patricians from Colonel Pyncheon of the 17th century to Judge Pyncheon of the 19th on the one hand; on the other hand, Matthew Maule, the carpenter of the 17th century, and his disguised descendant who now calls himself Holgrave and is a daguerreotypist, takes photographs, which Hawthorne regards with some suspicion.

Cooper was faced with a dilemma in the *Littlepage Trilogy*[4] when it came to the question of the empty tenancy agitation in upstate New York which took place from 1839 to 1845, a matter of a fight between the tenants and the landlords. How could he bring in here his angle about original wrong? History provided him a little gimmick, because apparently the tenants dressed themselves up in order not to be apprehended later; as they raided the houses, burned the farms, burned the farmhouses, they dressed themselves in calico and paint. In *The Redskins*, you may recall, the tenants disguised themselves as Red Indians hoping that afterwards the destruction could all be set down to an Indian raid, and Cooper played around with the episode so that he could get in his idea about restitution being made to the originally dispossessed people. Now Hawthorne's novel is also a novel about levelling democracy, but the difference is not merely that Hawthorne is unequivocally for those people who are being levelled upwards, unlike Cooper, who is ambiguous. The more important point already mentioned is that Hawthorne deals with what I can only call class, class from the beginning, unlike Cooper, who came to this idea much later.

At the end of the novel, if you remember, although the Pyncheons have got hold of the House of the Seven Gables, Hawthorne suggests that from the outset – and I like this reference, from the outset – the Maules had their revenge because the Pyncheons had a claim to certain eastern lands, and of course they could never redeem this claim. The land had been taken over by squatters like Cooper's Thousandacres[5] and they had already got possession of a much bigger piece of property than the House of the Seven Gables. So Hawthorne is not saying democracy occurred with Jackson,[6] Hawthorne is not saying that democracy occurred in America in 1840 or 1845, what he is saying in the resolution of *The House of the Seven Gables* is that now, not only have the lands gone to the common tillers of the soil, but even the property of the Pyncheons becomes a joint heritage of the merged families. Holgrave marries Phoebe, and therefore every class conflict is over and now they will jointly enjoy all material comfort.

This ending has dissatisfied many readers, including the person I consider the shrewdest and the most sympathetic critic of the novel, Matthiessen, who complains that 'in the poetic justice of bestowing opulence on all those who had previously been deprived of it . . . Hawthorne overlooked the fact that he was sowing all over again the same seeds of evil' (332). I am not sure that Matthiessen is doing justice to Hawthorne. As I read the novel and the resolution, Hawthorne is saying so far, so good. He is not saying anything more. He is saying relative justice has been done. With regard to what he is saying about its finished quality as justice for all time to come,

I think what we have to do is to see his ironic treatment of the representative of this levelling democracy, Holgrave. I have already quoted to you a passage about Holgrave where Hawthorne says 'as to the better centuries, may we never live to doubt it'. But Holgrave's error lay in the fact that he thought his century more than any past or future one was going to, and I want to quote this again, 'exchange the tattered garments of Antiquity for a brand new suit'.

To this I may add a few other comments, such as Hawthorne's authorial comment that there was something about Holgrave, 'not sinister but questionable' (Ch. 10, 337), and he does question it, he does question it in this book and later. Or the following again about Holgrave but more in his representative capacity, and I like to cite this because it picks up the clothes idea, clothes imagery, sartorial imagery, the suit of antiquity, the tattered garments of antiquity and a new suit. Talking of Holgrave, Hawthorne says, 'his career it would be difficult to pre-figure'. That is his reference to the future, and it is nowhere nearly as unambiguous as Matthiessen takes it to be:

> His career it would be difficult to pre-figure . . . these matters are delightfully uncertain. . . . Like certain chintzes, calicoes and ginghams, they [that is, people like Holgrave, the new democracy, rising democracy] show finely in their first newness, but cannot stand the sun and rain, and assume a very sober aspect after washing-day.
>
> (Ch. 12, 351–2)

And I suggest that at least you consider whether in fact even *The House of the Seven Gables*, which is a novel about restitution, setting right an old wrong, whether even this novel has the quality of finished-ness, or whether even within this novel itself as regards the centuries to come, we do not have a question mark. That is why I said the questionable quality of Holgrave in democracy, the problematic nature of its future, is, I suggest, taken up in *The Blithedale Romance*.

The story thus is not finished according to me in *The House of the Seven Gables*. It is taken up I think via the opposition between Boston and Blithedale or 19th-century reality as Hawthorne saw it, knew it, lived in it, and a utopian idea of socialism. We overlook this aspect of intellectual exploration and even some practical experiments in America of the 19th century, his Boston realities and this utopian idea of socialism as made available to Hawthorne not merely by European thinkers, though we have that European reference again in Hawthorne. Unlike many other American writers I can think of, Hawthorne sees that these things are not the creation of the American forest. He would point to the continuities accessible to him through the early European socialist thinkers, Robert Owen or Fourier or Saint-Simon,[7] and of course by his own personal experience with Ripley's Brook Farm.[8]

First again, the idea of continuity, Hawthorne's awareness as I suggested of the larger continuity with European problems and possibilities, but more important, the sense of continuity with the American past itself: the 17th-century Puritan idea as narrated in the first chapters of Bradford's *Plymouth Colony* of a cooperative commonwealth, cooperative land farming experiments, that is how they started out; and of course it broke up pretty quickly. There are numerous direct and indirect references to this 17th-century experiment; I shall cite only one: Coverdale's description of himself and other Blithedalers, Blithedaleans, as 'the descendants of the Pilgrims, whose high enterprises . . . we had taken up, and were carrying it onward and aloft, to a point which they never dreamed of attaining' (Ch. 14, 508).

This is to me a very complicated book. It once occurred to me that if one thought of Hawthorne's trilogy as a series of three plays, one could say: *The Scarlet Letter* is a tragedy, *The House of the Seven Gables* a historico-political comedy, and *The Blithedale Romance* a historico-political problem play. *The Blithedale Romance* looks backward at the connection between Blithedale and 17th-century radical ideas and movements as well as forward to a new 'point' which is, of course, socialism. For Hawthorne's disclaimer in the Preface notwithstanding, utopian socialism is the subject of *The Blithedale Romance* and its examination is both subtle and searching.

Of course, among the foundation ideas of the Blithedale community there are some which have nothing to do with socialism, such as the privileging of the agricultural over other forms of life and activity. The novel ridicules and rejects such ideas. As for essentialist socialist ideas, principles and basic motivations, the novel neither ridicules nor endorses but *examines* them.

The Blithedale Romance invites readers not to emote but to think, to consider, to think and consider for himself or herself. There is a sort of Brechtian strategy at work, a sort of non-sentimental coolness and hardness. Roland Barthes would categorize it as a 'readerly' rather than 'writerly' text[9] and Bakhtin as 'dialogic' rather than 'monologic'.[10] The book follows no single stream of either thought or attitude or narrative but provides, instead, multiple perspectives from various standpoints on the total idea-entity of Blithedale, or socialism, as well as on its several necessary practical and theoretical implications. In the novel's last chapter, long years after the narrator has left and done with the Blithedale experiment, he says posterity may wish to dig up its history and profit by it. And I do believe that even contemporary students of socialism or socialisms will find points and insights of profit in this novel of early socialism by Hawthorne.

There is no question about the force with which the vision that animates those who join the Blithedale experiment, the goal towards which they strive, is presented, nor any ambiguity about the distribution of sympathies as between the values avowed by the Blithedaleans and those which govern 'the iron framework of society' which they have left behind. Coverdale and the other visionaries assert the principle of human brotherhood as against 'the false and cruel principles on which human society has all along been based' (Ch. 3, 449). It is only when the members of the Blithedale experiment themselves turn out to be men of iron masquerading as visionaries that Blithedale is dismissed as a sham – as false as society, but more hypocritical. It is finally judged, not by the standards and norms of society, but in terms of its own professed values, and it deserved to die, the narrator observes, for its 'infidelity to its own higher spirit' (Ch. 29, 584).

The Blithedale Romance is a critique and, of its many critical perspectives on socialism, I will point to only two. One is universalist as articulated by Hollingsworth, one of the main characters, in the following statement: 'there is not human nature in it' (Ch. 15, 517). The other, more consistent, and, I think, more important critique is historical, having to do with the realities of time and place, and the consequent incongruities of motivation, consciousness and purpose. The dominant images and impressions are of 'an illusion, a masquerade, a pastoral, a counterfeit Arcadia, in which . . . grown-up men and women [are] making a play-day' (Ch. 3, 451).

In his Preface Hawthorne describes Blithedale in a wonderful phrase as 'essentially a day-dream, and yet a fact' (439). This is a historicist critique. All facts are not realities in the historical sense. The question is not whether Blithedale is good or bad but, in the final analysis, whether it is real. And the novel's most pervasive as well as most explicitly stated judgement is that Blithedale is *not* real. It is pure romancing. But why?

The answer mentioned earlier can always be one possible answer: 'there is not human nature in it'. But another answer has to do with Blithedale as utopian, not as to human nature but as to historical evolution. It is utopia – no place – because it is out of place and out of time. As the narrator puts it explicitly:

> But, considered in a profounder relation, it was part of another age, a different state of society, a segment of an existence peculiar in its aims and methods, a leaf of some mysterious volume interpolated into the current history which time was writing off.
>
> (Ch. 17, 525)

The Blithedale Romance is thus not so much a 'romance' as a book whose *subject* is romance and whose critique of utopian socialism is precisely that it is utopian, 'a fact' which yet when seen through historical realism turns out to be 'essentially a day-dream'. In other words, what Hawthorne insists on from first to last is precisely the utopian nature of utopian socialism. So far from making Blithedale plausible or emphasizing its here-and-now existence, he shows it up instead for what it is: a 'romantic' illusion, something unhistorically conceived and therefore unreal in the age of buoyant individualism and liberal democracy. The age itself, however, is seen in still larger historical terms which constitute the final or at least the framing perspective of the book, the sense of history beyond current history which includes the past as well as the future. From the perspective of 19th-century Boston, Blithedale may appear to be shadowy and insubstantial. But there is, nevertheless, the insistence that it is worthy of critical consideration, that it may have something to offer to the future. And this is precisely what Coverdale the narrator attempts to do when he concludes in the last chapter: 'More and more I feel that we had struck upon what ought to be a truth. Posterity may dig it up, and profit by it'.

Profit by it – as from a bad example, as something to be avoided? Or, as something to be learnt from so as to improve upon it the next time? *Ought* to be a truth – but is not or was not, then, in the existing state of the world? But might be for a future generation and a future time?

Hawthorne leaves his readers with these teasing ambiguities, and I will conclude by saying that the fact that in three slender works of fiction he examined such issues of the modern world as democracy, individual freedom, the status of women, the problems and possibilities of liberal democracy as well as socialism, speaks volumes for the historical and sociological grasp of an author known chiefly as a writer of romances.

Notes

1 William Bradford (1590–1627), English Puritan separatist who moved to Leiden in Holland to escape persecution from King James I and then emigrated to Plymouth Colony on the *Mayflower* in 1620. He served as governor of the colony intermittently for thirty years. His journal, *Of Plymouth Plantation*, covered the years 1620–47.

2 Ralph Waldo Emerson (1803–82), American essayist, lecturer, philosopher and poet who led the Transcendentalist movement of the mid-19th century which critiqued the conformity of contemporary society and urged everyone to find an original relationship to the universe. He was seen as the champion of individualism and emphasized self-reliance and independence.

3 Mikhail Bakhtin (1895–1975), Russian philosopher and literary critic who worked on literary theory, ethics and the philosophy of language. His *The Dialogic Imagination*, published in 1975, is a compilation of four essays which introduce the concepts of *heteroglossia* ('primacy of context over text'), *dialogism* ('dialogic' work carries on a dialogue with other works of literature and

other authors, informs and is informed by previous works, listening is dialogic and living is participating in dialogue) and *chronotope* ('time space', the connectedness of temporal and spatial relationships).

4 The three novels that constitute Cooper's *Littlepage Trilogy – Satanstoe* (1845), *The Chainbearer* (1845) and *The Redskins* (1846) – are novels of social protest concerned with the ownership of land and the Anti-Rent agitation aimed at ending land tenancy in New York State, which represented an important episode in the transition from Jeffersonian Republicanism to Jacksonian populist democracy.

5 Aaron Thousandacres in *The Chainbearer* is a squatter who argues against absentee landlordism and for a labour theory of value.

6 Andrew Jackson (1767–1845), American soldier and statesman who served as a general in the United States Army and in both houses of the United States Congress before being elected the seventh president of the United States (1829–37). He sought to advance the rights of the common man against a corrupt aristocracy.

7 Robert Owen (1771–1837), Welsh textile manufacturer, philanthropist, social reformer, a founder of utopian socialism and the co-operative movement, promoted experimental socialistic communities and tried to improve working conditions for his factory workers.

Charles Fourier (1772–1837) and Claude Henri de Rouvray, Comte de Saint-Simon (1760–1825), both French and founders of utopian socialism. Fourier, an early socialist thinker, influenced Marx and his social and moral views have become mainstream thinking today. Saint-Simon, a political and economic theorist and businessman, stated that the essential requirements of the industrial or working class needed to be recognized and fulfilled and thus inspired utopian socialism.

8 Ripley's Brook Farm was a utopian experiment in communal living in the 1840s in the United States founded by a former Unitarian minister, George Ripley, and his wife, Sophia, nine miles from Boston in Massachusetts, and was partly inspired by Transcendentalism.

9 Roland Barthes (1915–80), French literary theorist, philosopher, critic and semiotician who influenced structuralism and post-structuralism. Most texts, he argues, are 'readerly' texts presented in a linear, traditional manner; meaning is predetermined and the reader is a 'site' to receive information. 'Writerly' texts require the active participation of the reader in establishing the meaning of the text; meaning is not fixed or stable, and, whether consciously or unconsciously, writing is an ideological act.

10 See Note 3.

Works cited

Bakhtin, Mikhail. *The Dialogic Imagination: Four Essays*. Ed. Michael Holquist. Tr. Caryl Emerson and Michael Holquist. Austin: University Press, 1981.

Barthes, Roland. *The Pleasure of the Text*. Tr. Richard Miller with a note by Richard Howard. New York: Hill and Wang, 1975.

Bradford, William. *Of Plymouth Plantation 1620–1647*. Ed. Samuel Eliot Morison. New York: Knopf, 1959.

Cooper, James Fenimore. *The Redskins, Indian and Injin, Conclusion of the Littlepage Manuscripts*. New York: Burgess & Stringer, 1846.

———. *Satanstoe, or, the Littlepage Manuscripts*. New York: W.A. Townsend, 1860.

———. *The Chainbearer, or, the Littlepage Manuscripts*. Chicago: Clarke Bedford, 1885.

Eliot, T.S. 'The Hawthorne Aspect'. *The Little Review*, August 1918. Quoted in *Hawthorne: A Collection of Critical Essays*. Ed. with an Introduction by A. N. Kaul. Twentieth Century Views. Englewood Cliffs: Prentice-Hall Inc., 1966.

Emerson, Ralph Waldo. *The Complete Writings of Ralph Waldo Emerson*. 2 Vols. New York: W.H. Wise & Co., 1929.

Hawthorne, Nathaniel. *The Complete Novels and Selected Tales of Nathaniel Hawthorne*. Ed. with an Introduction by Norman Holmes Pearson. New York: The Modern Library, 1937.

———. 'Endicott and the Red Cross', 1014–18. *The Blithedale Romance*, 435–585. *The House of the Seven Gables*, 243–436. 'The Maypole of Merry Mount', 882–90. *The Scarlet Letter*, 85–240. *The Complete Novels and Selected Tales of Nathaniel Hawthorne*. Ed. with an Introduction by Norman Holmes Pearson. New York: The Modern Library, 1937.

James, Henry. *Hawthorne*. English Men of Letters Series. London: Macmillan, 1879.

Matthiessen, Francis Otto. *American Renaissance: Art and Expression in the Age of Emerson and Whitman*. New York: Oxford University Press, 1941.

Mills, Charles Wright. *The Sociological Imagination*. Oxford and New York: Oxford University Press, 1959, rpt. 2000.

Winters, Yvor. *'Maule's Curse': Seven Studies in the History of American Obscurantism*. Norfolk, CO: New Directions, 1938.

Yeats, William Butler. '"Among School Children" and "Sailing to Byzantium"'. *Selected Poetry*. Ed. with an Introduction by Norman Jeffares. London and Basingstoke: Macmillan, 1962.

Index